Inspi
Women

Prepared for Spiritual Battle

Anne Le Tissier

Published 2008 by CWR, Waverley Abbey House, Waverley Lane, Farnham, Surrey GU9 8EP, UK. Registered Charity No. 294387. Registered Limited Company No. 1990308.

See back of book for list of National Distributors.

Unless otherwise indicated, all Scripture references are from the Holy Bible: New International Version (NIV), copyright © 1973, 1978, 1984 by the International Bible Society.
The Message: Scripture taken from *The Message*. Copyright © 1993, 1994,1995, 1996, 2000, 2001, 2002. Used by permission of NavPress Publishing Group.

Concept development, editing, design and production by CWR

Cover image: Getty Images/Photodisc/ballyscanlon

Printed in Finland by WS Bookwell

ISBN: 978-1-85345-471-4

Contents

Introduction

'For our struggle is not against flesh and blood, but against
the rulers, against the authorities, against the powers of
this dark world and against the spiritual forces of evil in the
heavenly realms.'

Ephesians 6:12

Some years ago, I watched the futuristic film *The Matrix*.
It tells the intriguing story of Neo, a computer hacker who
discovers his perceived world is little more than a virtual-
reality simulation. In fact, almost every human being is
imprisoned in this colossal computer-generated dream world,
unaware that a ruling class of robotic machines are extracting
their very life energy in order to generate electrical power.

I admit it's a little far-fetched, and yet it offers an interesting
glimpse into how Satan schemes to drain our own lives of power
by concealing spiritual realities from the reality of the world.

Neo is asked how he would define 'real'. He was challenged
that if all that is 'real' is simply that which he can experience
through his physical senses – sight, sound, touch, taste and
smell – then 'real' is merely electrical signals received and
deciphered by the brain.[1]

It's a poignant question, especially when we're bombarded
by a 'seeing is believing' culture – where spiritual realities are
disregarded as fairy-tale myth, or deemed unnecessary clutter in
the pursuit of tangible success and achievement. And the more
we're immersed in the material realm, the more our lives are
unwittingly sapped of the potential spiritual power that is ours
in Christ. But as much as it may be a struggle at times to sustain
our spiritual focus, it's imperative if we want to take ground in

the ongoing spiritual battle with Satan's forces of evil.

There is an abundance of good books available on casting out demons, territorial spirits and exorcism, so I haven't attempted to write yet another. But if I could invent a pair of spectacles which enabled us to see with our physical eyes the battle being fought in the spiritual realm, we might well be astounded by its relentless intensity, its strategic aim and even its focus on our personal lives. Unfortunately, such specs don't exist but I can, I hope, reawaken our perception of spiritual reality and remind us of the nature of our spiritual battle; the training and armour that equips us to overcome demoralising and distracting behaviour embraced by the world, the character and power of our enemy, and how we might prepare to take an effective stand against him. After all, no one in their right mind walks casually across a live battlefield as if nothing were happening – at best, they'd soon be surrounded and imprisoned; at worst, they'd be shot down.

Neo had to acknowledge and understand both the realm of a mere simulation and the realm outside the computer program, in order to conquer the enemy machines. Similarly, we need to heighten our awareness of the battle for God's righteousness in the spiritual realm, that we may experience Christ's victory while living in the secular world. And so, if we accept the truth of Ephesians 6:12, I trust that this book will help us to put that belief into further action.

Anne Le Tissier, 2008

Chapter 1

To be or not to be …
a soldier

'… choose for yourselves this day whom you will serve, whether the gods your forefathers served beyond the River, or the gods of the Amorites, in whose land you are living. But as for me and my household, we will serve the LORD.'
Joshua 24:15

Nestled into the sofa with my feet outstretched, toasting in front of a roaring fire, the cosy glow of a memorable evening abruptly turned cold as a friend froze my heart with his bold declaration: 'Anne, you are not a Christian.'

I was fourteen.

Brought up by a staunch atheist and a lapsed Methodist, church attendance had been a rare occurrence. Nevertheless, my schooling provided Christian-based assemblies where I'd learnt a number of hymns, listened to Scripture and heard endless stories on how to live a caring, moral life. As a child, I also loved spending Sunday mornings alone with my parents' record player, singing along to the musical *Jesus Christ Superstar*;[1] in fact, I listened to it so many times I can still recall most of the lyrics.

Scanty as my religious input had been, however, I had decided I believed in God, imagining Him as some might picture a fairy-tale wizard. He was a thin, wrinkly man with a tangled mane of wispy hair, beady eyes gleaming above a long grey beard, stooping shoulders draped with a lengthy mottled robe and, leaning against a wooden staff, he surveyed the world from a fluffy white cloud. I also believed there was a man called Jesus whose birth in a stable we celebrate with parties, presents and tinsel, and whose death and resurrection we vaguely recall amongst foil-wrapped chocolate eggs. I'd even heard of a holy ghost, but it sounded too weird and spooky to want to find out more.

This fairy-tale faith and the occasional spate of urgent 'help me' prayers was all my belief amounted to. Hence, my friend's boldness was both timely and true. I was upset – angry, in fact – and argued that I was indeed a Christian, only to hear that it meant far more than mere belief in God: it implied a conscious decision to ask for forgiveness, to submit to Jesus

Christ as Lord, and to begin to live a life that the Holy Spirit would guide, discipline and nurture in line with God's ways, God's purposes and God's overall plan for my life.

Angry as I was, my attention had been caught and I determined to prove my friend wrong. But the subsequent weeks of soul-searching and inner turmoil led me on a journey that proved him right, one which began by trying out a church – 'and the rest,' as they say, 'is history'!

So why am I sharing my story in a book about spiritual battle? Because that was the point when I effectively switched sides. Up until my actual conversion when I gave my life to Jesus, I believed in God but remained captive to an unseen spiritual enemy. From the moment I was reconciled to God, however, through accepting Christ's Lordship and His sacrifice for my sins, two things happened: I became a citizen of heaven, and I unwittingly signed up for God's army; conscripted for military service in the ongoing spiritual battle between my King and His enemy.

I understood the implications of the first point at once – I was no longer going to end up in hell, I had a new relationship to develop, a life to be transformed and a job to do for Jesus. As for joining an army, however, that realisation took much longer to evolve and some years before it was actually put into practice.

A soldier in name but not in practice
'... faith by itself, if it is not accompanied by action, is dead' (James 2:17).

Sometime after my commitment, I found myself reading the scriptural analogy of being a good soldier and fighting the good fight (2 Tim. 2:3; 1 Tim. 6:12); terms that suggested I'd find myself in a battle. I was also keen to understand the meaning of what I'd heard other Christians call 'spiritual warfare', so I began reading books on intercession, prayer warfare, territorial spirits, exorcism and suchlike.

I learnt quite a lot about the subject – in theory – but apart from a quick dabble in prayer here and there, I wasn't really getting involved myself. As a young member of an intercessory group, I'd listen to others taking their prayerful stand against the demonic realm but felt personally inadequate to do so; felt that I was too young, too ungodly, that I lacked sufficient scriptural knowledge, that I still didn't really understand how to pray despite reading all those books and, if I'm honest, feared what would happen if a demon actually manifested while I was praying against it.

That fear wasn't entirely wrong as there are aspects of the battle (exorcism, for example), in which we oughtn't to participate without mature spiritual discernment and prayerful support. But it was still some time before I appreciated my need to take a stand as Christ's soldier in every attitude and circumstance, rather than just leaving it to prayer meetings.

'Warfare' in the spiritual realm is more than a scriptural metaphor, it is a daily reality whether we choose to accept it for ourselves or delegate it to men and women who have a special interest in the subject. It affects us no matter our age, background, intellect or even our ability to find the books of the minor prophets hiding amongst the pages of the Old Testament! In fact, the battle in the spiritual realm is a reality for everyone, regardless of their belief in the one true God.

To be or not to be Christ's soldier, therefore, is purely dependent on whose side of the battle we are on. There can be no pacifists in this spiritual war; this is not a spectator sport – conscription into God's army is obligatory on becoming a citizen of heaven. That said, we can become so entwined with the visible we can lose touch with the invisible, so before we take this any further, I'd like to take a moment to recall how it all started ...

Are you sitting comfortably? Then I'll begin!

The nature of the battle

'... thanks be to God! He gives us the victory through our Lord Jesus Christ. Therefore, my dear [sisters], stand firm. Let nothing move you ...' (1 Cor. 15:57–58).

Once upon an eternity there was and is and will always be a holy kingdom whose ruler is God. With divine delight He lovingly created angels and people to serve Him and enjoy His kingdom.

One timeless day, an important angel (whom we now call Satan), grew disgruntled as he mused on his longing to be worshipped and revered as king and, with cunning deception enticed some other angels to transfer their allegiance. But being incapable of overpowering God's warriors they set off from their heavenly home to establish their own 'kingdom' on earth.

Now the earth was a most beautiful creation, perfectly designed to nurture God's people. Tragically, however, through suggestion, contradiction, seduction and assertion against God's perfect word, works and will, Satan, being masked as a serpent, enticed them into joining his rebellious subjects. The true King was heartbroken but He loved His children far too much to leave them in Satan's captivity. And so, from that moment, a battle ensued to save humankind from the enemy's dominion of death.

And what a battle it turned out to be!

There came a man, born in Israel by miraculous divine conception. The Messiah – God's very own Son – came into the world to save us from Satan's doom, once and for all. Oh, how Satan schemed to destroy that man before He could restore the human race to their heavenly home; how he fought to kill and curb the divine strategy to save them from sin. But Jesus, our Lord and King, cried out in triumph from the horrors of the cross: 'It is finished.' Satan's hold on the souls of men and women was eternally broken by Christ's perfect life, His once-for-all perfect sacrifice, and His subsequent victory over death ...

It's tempting to leave this story on its high note and forget about the defeated foe. But it hasn't finished yet. Although Christ has the spiritual victory for all who put their faith in Him, we're still caught up in a ferocious conflict against an enraged enemy, for a period of God's choosing until Satan's final demise.

The war rages on between good and evil for the hearts and minds of humankind; a battle against an adversary who blinds countless people to God's truth. Daily we witness the havoc and destruction Satan's kingdom deploys on this world and his strategies to demoralise life and faith. But as powerfully deceptive as Satan may be, he fears the authority Christ has given His people, and will use any means he can muster to undermine the potential power we might otherwise use against him; he'll sow seeds of ignorance, unbelief, apathy and fear, or simply distract us from warfare.

As soldiers of Christ, we live in the physical but wage war in the spiritual (2 Cor. 10:3–4); we share our lives with secular society while appropriating (taking possession of) Christ's victory in the heavenly realms. And we're all on an equal footing before our High King and Commander whether we feel on a par with a first-day cadet, lieutenant or brigadier. We may have more or less Christian experience than our neighbour, but our ability to take our stand only arises from Christ's power within. As soon as we think we're somehow good enough, wise enough or talented enough to take part in spiritual battle then we've missed the point completely.

There is nothing clever or 'super-spiritual' about prayer warfare. It's a battle we're all going to face to some degree or other. Some will be led to oppose demonic forces possessing a non-believer's life, some will find themselves standing against a territorial spirit, but all of us will daily be confronted by the bombardment of Satan's evil dominion and tempted to follow his ways rather than God's. And our response to that is as much an act of warfare as the casting out of demons.

Proving our oath of allegiance

'And the people said to Joshua, "We will serve the LORD our God and obey him"' (Josh. 24:24).

In his book, *To Be a Soldier*, Richard O'Connor explains how the British Army, at the time of publication (1996), was facing extreme pressure owing to falling recruitment figures, a lower standard of new recruits and increasing resignations.[2] Sadly, however, this might describe God's army, if we fail to accept the part we must play, or train for our role in spiritual battle.

New army cadets take an oath of allegiance at an informal ceremony; an oath before Almighty God promising their loyalty to serve the king or queen of England, to defend them against all enemies and obey their orders. Only then does the training start, and in time they're passed out as ready for action, be that wartime combat or providing disaster relief. But they can't take their oath then return home and forget all about it.

Likewise, our submission to Christ requires an active response. We too shall be called on to prove our faith with the good deeds required of being Christ's soldier; of caring for the sick and suffering or providing for the poor – but we shall never leave the war zone. And so our faith continues to be proved through the inevitable 'deed' of battle; of combat in the heavenly realms, each and every day.

This then is how we prove our allegiance, not by means of ceremonial declaration, but through lives lived in loyalty to God's righteousness with unquestioning obedience to His command and a willingness to fight for His kingdom. Our training will continue throughout our lives as we prepare for daily battle, our armour will feel more comfortable the more we get used to wearing it and our weapons technique will be honed with practice as we discern each strategic battle plan. Therefore, 'you, [woman] of God ... pursue righteousness, godliness, faith, love, endurance and gentleness. Fight the good fight of the faith. Take hold of the eternal life to which you were called when you made your good confession in the presence of many witnesses' (1 Tim. 6:11–12).

Let's shake off any fear or apathy the enemy has induced and rejoin the ranks of God's valiant warriors. And remember, as Christian soldiers we have a distinct advantage: we're fighting on the winning side against a defeated foe!

For reflection

• I assume from the fact you're reading this book that you already believe in a battle between good and evil, but to what extent do you perceive yourself as being caught up in it?

• Do you delegate the role of soldier to those you believe have a penchant for prayer warfare, thereby excusing yourself from God's army, let alone frontline attack?

- Is your life geared more towards good deeds or spiritual battle? God seeks both in His soldiers. How might you redress any imbalance?

- In the past the Army has been criticised for its advertising campaigns, with many people feeling they give a glamourised and unrealistic view of military life and fail to point out the disadvantages.[3]

  - When sharing your faith with an unbeliever, are you tempted to paint a rosy picture of Christian life, promoting the potential peace, healing, provision and fulfilment but ignoring that Jesus also promised trouble? If so, might this disillusion new converts when their new-found faith is rocked by difficult circumstances?

  - In light of this, how might you explain the implications that becoming a Christian includes automatic entry into God's army (as opposed to God's social club or pleasure park) without frightening off a new child of God with dark imagery of the satanic realm?

Let's pray …

Forgive me, Lord, where I've let You down, pottering on the sidelines of faith rather than marching out in the confidence of my salvation, prepared to stand my ground for Your kingdom of righteousness. But now, as for me, I will prepare to serve You as a soldier in Your army of light.

Chapter 2

One world, two realms

'Since, then, you have been raised with Christ, set your hearts on things above, where Christ is seated at the right hand of God. Set your minds on things above, not on earthly things. For you died, and your life is now hidden with Christ in God.'
Colossians 3:1–3

Relaxing in the bath one evening, I looked back on my day off with satisfaction. I had breezed through the queue-less supermarket, I'd dismantled, sanded down and varnished a second-hand sewing box, then warmed myself in the late afternoon sun repotting my collection of cacti. Yes, it had been a good day; peaceful, productive, restful and enjoyable – battle couldn't have been further from my mind.

There are days, however, when everything seems to be going wrong. Days when I'm crushed to read of a teenage suicide, when I hear of cancer, marriage breakdown and job loss in the lives of three friends, or when I can't shift the burden of a personal problem distracting my mind from my work. I'd like to say that on those days the effects of physical suffering alert me to the spiritual battle – and they do sometimes, but not always. In fact, it can have the opposite effect, tempting me into the temporary comforts of the here and now – immersing myself in 'busyness', the biscuit tin or a call to a sympathetic ear – rather than face up to reality.

Paul's teaching is quite clear: '… our struggle is not against flesh and blood … ' (Eph. 6:12). Somehow we need to develop our daily focus on the unseen spiritual battle while still living life in the physical realm. We don't want to ignore spiritual realities, but neither do we want to get so engrossed as to lose touch with the tangible reality of daily life. I love the special times of spiritual intimacy with God as I'm sure you do too, but as soldiers we also need to be aware of what's happening around us; seeing, hearing and perceiving situations with God's eyes and heart – discerning what Satan is up to that we may take our stand against him.

So let's take a look at both the visible and the invisible realms of God's world, to help us develop a healthy perspective, rather than live our lives at one end of the scale.

The visible physical realm

'In the beginning God created the heavens and the earth … God saw all that he had made, and it was very good …' (Gen. 1:1,31).

I believe God wants us to enjoy the physical realm; after all, He created it for us! As I recently enjoyed time out on my husband's sabbatical to walk the Cotswold Way and back (204 miles of exquisite scenery and invigorating hill climbs between Chipping Campden and Bath), I sensed in my spirit the extent of God's delight in my spontaneous response to the awesome escarpment views, the variety of wildlife, delicate flowers, majestic trees, fresh unpolluted air, the exhilaration of hilltop windy ridges and the stillness of gentle brooks. But He also delights in our appreciation of music, art, sunsets, technology, books, birdlife, sport, gardens and, of course, relationships with other people – all of which He created or inspired for our fulfilment, purpose and pleasure.

And the wonderful thing with the physical realm is the ease with which we enjoy it. Through sight, sound, smell, touch and taste we use our physical senses to absorb and engage with our tangible environment; rouge-swathed horizons, carpets of golden leaves, frost-encrusted pine trees, freshly baked bread, a long hot soak in a bubbly bath, twittering hedge sparrows, bleating lambs, walking barefoot over sand or grass, the scourge of an east wind on rosy cheeks, fine wine and gourmet food, a steaming pot of coffee, the crackle and flicker of an open fire, the full-bodied fungal odour permeating woodland paths …

Needless to say, there are also plentiful ways we experience the uglier side of life on this earth which we needn't list here, but God loved that which He made and His love does not change (just take a look at Psalm 104 to glimpse God's satisfaction, inspiring the psalmist's praise). He must grieve for the sin that has raped His creation of innocence, purity, beauty and harmony, but it still delights His heart when His children are amazed by His wonderful works, when they appreciate or share His creative gifts, and take responsibility for that which He's entrusted to their care.

And so I believe God wants us to enjoy the tangible realm and to use our intellect, talents and relationships, but we do need to keep it in balance with the reality of the spiritual realm. After all, any 'worldly' power or success we achieve is temporary, proving quite useless in the spiritual realm; whereas the power of the risen Lord Jesus made available to us in that realm enables us to take our stand against evil spirits and equips us to bear lasting fruit as we interact with all that we can see. And if the invisible realm is where the ultimate power lies, then that is surely the ultimate reality.

The invisible heavenly realm

'And God raised us up with Christ and seated us with him in the heavenly realms in Christ Jesus' (Eph. 2:6).

If Paul wrote us a letter in which He praised the Lord for giving us a millionaire's inheritance from long-lost Aunty Flo, the cancellation of our mortgage debt or the new-found cure for our loved one's fatal illness, I feel sure we'd be hugging the postman, jumping for joy and joining Paul with shouts of praise to God. But do we get as excited to hear that He has 'blessed us in the heavenly realms with every spiritual blessing in Christ' (Eph. 1:3)? If you're like me, then somehow it doesn't hit the spot with quite the same impact. But Paul truly engaged with it, and therefore sought to live his new life in Christ from God's eternal perspective (Gal. 2:19–20), and it's on these heavenly realms we also need to set our sights.

This place, though unseen to the human eye, is the spiritual environment where the forces of good and evil battle to win control over human hearts (Eph. 6:12). Without the protection of Christ's perfect blood it's a dangerous place to go, but we who believe and are therefore in Christ may receive its spiritual blessings. These priceless heavenly gifts include an intimate relationship with God as Father, the infilling of the Holy Spirit, an awesome heavenly inheritance, the enabling of God's immense power, the comfort of His unconditional love, and purpose in life, just to name a few of those mentioned in Paul's letter. Furthermore, not one believer is excluded from these blessings.

I do hope that excites us, but it may yet be that although we believe in the power of these promised blessings, some of us don't feel we've experienced them to the extent Paul describes, while others may be too overwhelmed with the physical needs of life to get all that enthused. When we're suffering an incurable disease or our business is threatened with bankruptcy, 'heavenly realms' and 'spiritual blessings' may not seem like pressing priorities. And yet, absolutely nothing can ever hope to compare with such amazing promises, and it's only as we live in Christ and as we set our minds and hearts on this heavenly realm that we begin to appreciate their value and potential.

Simply knowing about God's immense power and purpose is one thing, but we need to know Christ and how to engage with His power if we want it to have any impact. Paul was able to face extreme physical hardship (irregular income, ill health, torture, imprisonment) because he learnt to live his physical life in the heavenly realms of spiritual blessings. His feet remained firmly on the ground but the reverent submission of his heart, mind, hands, feet, mouth and body became a fitting channel through which God could empower his life and impact the lives of countless others. Paul didn't disregard the hardships of life with irrelevant spirituality but was (and is) offering invaluable guidance to help us live a victorious life in Christ.

We cannot see Jesus with our physical eyes but as we learn to live life in the heavenly realms we can seek to know Him with the enlightened eyes of our heart. And this we do in order that we may begin to live in the power of those glorious spiritual blessings, no matter what difficult circumstances harass our earthly lives.

Redressing the balance

'Since we live by the Spirit, let us keep in step with the Spirit' (Gal. 5:25).

Maintaining an awareness of the heavenly realm in a material culture that pesters for our attention is quite possibly one of the most difficult areas to work on as we prepare for spiritual battle. I believe one of Satan's key strategies to limit our offensive battle is that of promoting the visible realm in order to distract us from the invisible – of making the most of our physical senses to the detriment of spiritual realities. But Paul also infers in his letter that to restore a balanced perspective, we need the Holy Spirit (Eph. 1:15–21).

I wonder how much we depend on the Spirit for our activities each day. If we're starting a new job, taking part in a church group or meeting, lacking physical strength or health for a task, or simply having too much to do in too little time, then we may well call out to God for the Holy Spirit's guidance and help. But what about the routine days – hours filled with familiar and usual expectations at work, when we're simply sitting and receiving in the congregation or home group, enjoying reasonable health and energy, or when the busyness of life is manageable? Do we cry out for help as passionately on those days as the others – if at all? Does our sense of physical ability annul the felt need for God's capability?

A great turning point came for me for me when I responded to the directive to live by the Spirit – to keep in step with the Spirit. It's a helpful, practical image of walking with Jesus, step by step, through every hour of the day; living by the Spirit – that is, listening to and responding to His prompts – with ever-increasing measure. And the reason it's been so poignant is that it keeps my heart focused on taking my stand against godlessness as I'm trained in God's ways of godliness; it increases my awareness of the spiritual realm as I live out my life in the physical realm.

This is an important truth to keep in mind as we move on to training camp in the next chapter. After all, the Holy Spirit is our 'drill instructor, strategist and weapons trainer'; it is He that prepares us for battle and equips us to take our stand. The more we listen to His spiritual instruction, the greater our awareness of the battle in which we live; the more we develop unconditional obedience, the greater our impact on destroying Satan's schemes.

Taking our first steps in the Spirit, however, is no easier than a toddler taking their first steps towards Mum; be prepared for lots of falls! But the more we practise, the more accustomed we become to walking with the perpetual awareness of the Holy Spirit's presence and the daily dependence on the Spirit's empowering. In fact, that's a key difference between training for a nation's army and training for God's army. Platoon instructors stand and watch as cadets struggle in their own strength to learn new skills and develop new muscles they never knew they had; whereas our divine instructor calls out commands then assists our response and development from the inside. Our role is simply to obey, and we'll think more about that in subsequent pages.

Developing our walk with the Spirit is a lifelong process. Although I've been learning for some years, I'm still not immune to being sidetracked (in fact, I distinctly walked in the opposite direction during my late teens and early twenties!). So before we consider our spiritual training, perhaps I may share some personal testimony which I hope may help in redressing the balance of our perspective on these two realms.

... At home

In the summer of 2007, Britain encountered terrible flooding in certain regions. Only six months beforehand, my husband and I bought our very first home – in Worcestershire – the first place I could really call my own little nest. We'd spent weeks renovating what was an old and somewhat rundown property and had only just completed the sitting room when the floods hit. Living and working in Kent for the best part of the year, it was a call from our neighbour that alerted us to the problems in Worcestershire. But owing to impassable roads we were unable to travel up for over two days. Meanwhile, we watched the news with anguish as hundreds of families were displaced from the wreckage of their homes – reports of flood victims being airlifted from swamped stairwells and the tragedy of those who were swept away by tumultuous currents in their attempts to assist other people.

Those hours of waiting reminded me that our home is both temporary and material; caring for human need and the salvation of souls from Satan's dominion of death is of far greater importance than owning or establishing a home in this temporary life, as marvellous a gift from God as that can be. What could so easily have become a treasure on earth was poignantly put back in perspective. We live in what we call a 'fallen world' and experience the repercussions alongside our non-believing neighbours. But we have a much greater hope and security with which we can reach out, as we too suffer with them.[1]

... With loved ones

My perspective on relationships has also been challenged in a variety of ways, but let's take the example that I'm very close to my mother, who still lives in Guernsey. When we've spent precious time together on one of her visits, I face the upsetting dilemma of her having to return home, which accentuates my love and felt need for her. It begs the question as to whom I am most reliant upon for a sense of being loved, appreciated and cared for – my husband, family, close friends ... or God?

Physical touch is known to be vital for emotional wellbeing and Jesus may well express His compassionate understanding through our gentle touch or loving embrace of others where appropriate. Even so, our ultimate experience of perfect love can only come from our heavenly Father; there is no greater love than the Lord's.

... At work

As for my work, I long that it would be successful, but God has challenged me to question the meaning of success. Do I consider it in terms of the number of sales, financial reward and positive book reviews, or in the number of hearts who've been saved or who have deepened their relationship with God through the words I write?

We were created to fulfil God's purpose in our generation

and, for some of us, that includes the atmosphere of paid or voluntary employment, 'Christian' or secular, outside the home. There's nothing wrong with seeking to be the best that we can be, but God still weighs the motive in our hearts, and Scripture provides that motive's benchmark: that all that we are and do might be for the praise of God's glory, rather than our own.

... In everything

One morning I found myself feeling insecure and emotionally upset, so I talked with God about it in prayer. I felt led to specifically name all those things that I hold close to my heart: my husband, my daughter and son-in-law, my mother and immediate family, my church family, my little nest in Worcestershire, my health and so on. As I completed naming everything, I saw them all again in the truth and the light of eternity and was reminded they will all disappear from my life at some stage or another, and there's nothing I can do about it. 'Naked I came from my mother's womb, and naked I shall depart ...' (Job 1:21).

I trust that my life – my relationships, talents, responsibilities, possessions – will be used to impact others for God in some way, but of all those things precious to me, only God will remain constant and for ever, as part of my life both in time and in eternity. And that, if it helps, is just a tiny glimpse of what it means to keep my spiritual life in the right perspective and in balance with my physical life.

If we merely believe in God, and if all we perceive as reality is our homes, relationships, jobs and so on, then our lives risk becoming completely immersed in the material realm; one in which it can be quite a struggle to maintain our focus on the spiritual realm, let alone prepare ourselves for warfare. So let's remind ourselves daily that while we live in two realms, it's in the spiritual realm where we ultimately receive our power over Satan, that we may progress as soldiers of Christ and thereby take our victorious stand.

For reflection

• Does the life that you live in the physical realm overshadow the reality of the spiritual battle to the extent that it seems irrelevant, or simply not important enough to prioritise on your 'to do' list?

• What, if anything, keeps you preoccupied with the physical realm: overindulgence in leisure activities or sensual pleasures; an addiction to food, drink or television; the distraction of work and the pursuit of success; misplaced security in finances, home or relationships, for example? What action might you take to help restore your spiritual focus?

• Do you only think about battle during your personal devotions or a prayer meeting, or could there be other opportunities where God might reveal a battleground for prayer – for the person in front or behind you in a queue, while watching your children play or socialise with non-believing friends, while listening to the news or reading the newspaper, for example?

- Now in order to kill the enemy, our men must be roused to anger; that there be advantage from defeating the enemy, they must also have their rewards... so that all your men may have a keen desire to fight, each on his own account. Sun Tzŭ, circa 490 BC[2]

- Bearing in mind that Satan seeks to steal your peace, power and provision in Christ, and considering how he continues to blind your unsaved friends and family while wreaking havoc in this fallen world through power, greed, violence and persecution, are you inflamed with righteous anger? If not, consider once again the potential and powerful spiritual blessings that God promises you in Christ that you may be roused to battle against Satan's deceitful schemes.

Let's pray ...

Holy Spirit, I depend on You for my day. Only You can bear real and lasting fruit through my life; only You can help transform me into an ever-increasing likeness to Christ; only You can empower me for victory against Satan's spiritual forces of evil. Thank You that You are here to help me.

Chapter 3

Army training

'Everyone who competes in the games goes into strict training.
They do it to get a crown that will not last; but we do it
to get a crown that will last for ever.'
1 Corinthians 9:25

We were 110 miles into our Cotswold Way pilgrimage when torrential rains made short work of saturating our flimsy waterproofs. I'd felt increasingly fitter over the weeks as we gradually ticked off each section, but walk number nine pushed my stamina yet further. The rain began within five minutes of leaving the car and grew steadily worse as we trudged onwards. After more than two and a half hours of sodden, slippery hill-walking, I thought I'd reached my limit as I lost my rhythmic stride, plodding up a steep, muddy woodland path. My breathing went haywire, my thighs dragged like lead weights, and chilled exhaustion fired aches and pains through my calves, shoulders and back while my heart pounded furiously against my chest.

Slowly but surely, however, the gradient eased as we reached the plateau and my body returned to normal; the aches disappeared, I found my stride and my breathing and heartbeat resumed a comfortable rhythm. The rain persisted as we continued our walk but I was feeling exhilarated, despite the recent ordeal.

When I later resumed my working week behind a desk, with most evenings tied up in meetings, my fitness level soon declined. Not that it concerns me, but it is a startling reminder that unless I keep on walking in step with the ways of the Holy Spirit, the characteristics of Christ in my life will also start to decline. If I'm not pushing onwards with God then I'll soon start slipping backwards – there's no such thing as a 'stagnant in-between'! And as Paul reminded young Timothy, 'physical training is of some value, but godliness has value for all things, holding promise for both the present life and the life to come' (1 Tim. 4:8); helping us maintain our spiritual perspective and take our stand against Satan.

The gospel bursts with its message of grace, hope, freedom,

healing and unconditional love – a priceless gift to our broken society. Thoughts of 'discipline' and 'obedience', however, may have been tarnished by previous periods of strict, ascetic religiosity with its drab clothing, legalistic behaviour codes, condemnation of innocent pleasures and lives bereft of joy. But Jesus came to give life, and not as a mere token but life in all its fullness; and He sent the Holy Spirit to help us live that life, without whom we're unable to share His victory over life-sapping sin.

The Spirit brings peace and inner security but He also walks in the ways of God. And it's as we align our step with the Spirit that we learn the true meaning of discipline. It doesn't shame us, crush our personality or render us inadequate, rather it dovetails the physical and the spiritual, it liberates our lives in Christ, develops intimacy with God and enables us to experience His power with ever-increasing measure.

That is why training to be Christ's soldier revolves around personal disciplines which hone a righteous and godly life. And that's why we're going to training camp!

Welcome to army barracks!

'No discipline seems pleasant at the time, but painful ...' (Heb. 12:11).

Hours of lectures on map-reading, fieldcraft and small arms; unremitting physical exercises; cold, wet, appetite-stretching outdoor survival training; pernickety room inspections; fastidious weapons handling and interminable drill practice are some of the army disciplines that barrage young cadets. In just ten weeks, a bunch of timid, civvy-dressed young men and women arriving for their first day of training will be transformed in appearance, skills and behaviour. But the consequence of soldiers not responding goes farther than the reprimand of an extra hundred sit-ups or toilet cleaning duty for a week – it could ultimately determine between life and death.

Discipline is essential on the battlefield. Without it, delays in obeying commands, fumbling over weapons, lack of physical fitness or disunited manoeuvres weaken and put at risk both soldier and army alike. And so, it should come as no surprise that '… God disciplines us for our good …' (Heb. 12:10).

We may believe in Jesus but to be His soldier we must put that belief into action: actively submitting to the teaching and commands in our training manual – God's Word – that comes alive to our hearts as the Holy Spirit inspires it. For 'All Scripture is God-breathed and is useful for teaching, rebuking, correcting and training in righteousness, so that the [woman] of God may be thoroughly equipped for every good work' (2 Tim. 3:16–17).

Godly discipline may at times feel far from pleasant – forgiving when we feel bruised and hurt, showing love though we feel repelled, witnessing when we're mocked or misunderstood. But please don't lose heart. It's this very training that will strengthen our faith to cope with any and every circumstance, hone and refine the skills He's given us to employ in warfare, and unite us with other 'soldiers' as an effective force against evil. After all, being disciplined in God's holy ways is paramount when facing an unholy enemy.

And neither be discouraged when the desired effects don't appear overnight. A 'six-pack abdomen' Royal Marine physique only develops after gruelling hours on a bench press and miles of running through muddy tracks. A hotshot sniper takes weeks to know his weapon, train a steady hand and hone a 'bull's-eye' focus. And holiness will surely be refined as we learn to live by the Spirit.

Training in godliness

'... train yourself to be godly' (1 Tim. 4:7).

Physical fitness is essential for the soldiers' outdoor life in which they get hungry and tired or face the extremes of climatic conditions, while still having to think clearly and put their survival and battle skills into practice. The British Army evaluates fitness with Grade A representing the peak required by the infantry and Grade E the standard set for cadets by their fifth week of training. In order to pass the selection process, however, potential recruits need only achieve Grade P.[1]

What a relief that we don't need to prove our own fitness before or after joining God's army! But as cadets are trained physically to increase their effectiveness as soldiers, so God trains us to be godly; training which empowers us to live victoriously in Satan's territory and equips us for eternity.

The word 'train' stems from the Greek word 'to exercise'. In other words, godliness won't just materialise because we want it to happen or because we ask God to make it happen. It's something we need to actively pursue by disciplining our walk to that of the Holy Spirit.

Godliness inspires us to express God's holy character as we learn to live in the presence of His Spirit now and the presence of Himself for eternity. Such training requires discipline of the whole person: body, mind and spirit. It implies a responsibility to read, meditate upon and learn from Scripture (2 Tim. 3:16–17), to maintain and treat our bodies with the reverence God's temple deserves (1 Cor. 6:19), to fit 'every loose thought and emotion and impulse into the structure of life shaped by Christ' (2 Cor. 10:5, *The Message*), to tame our tongue from worldly speech (James 3:2–12), to conduct ourselves 'in a manner worthy of the gospel' (Phil. 1:27), and to pray and seek

God 'continually' (1 Thess. 5:17). And just as army training equips soldiers to take their part in humanitarian relief, so we are trained to remember those in prison and suffering ill-treatment (Heb. 13:3), to help the poor and oppressed (Prov. 31:9; Matt. 25:37–40; Rom.12:13).

We have a faithful instructor – the command of the Spirit to our conscience. All we have to do is obey.

Training in obedience
'If you love me, you will obey what I command' (John 14:15).

Watching film actors play cantankerous drill sergeants shouting abuse at a fumbling platoon is enough to put me off joining the army for life! But the stringent discipline imposed during early cadet training serves to instil unquestioning obedience to higher command; a prerequisite principle for the battlefield itself.

No training is going to prove successful unless we're also going to obey; a principle made more obvious, perhaps, if we can recall a historic battle scene, re-enacted in a film or depicted in an oil painting. These snapshots position commanding officers on nearby hilltops from where they surveyed the battle; a place where they could see the whole picture in order to formulate strategy. But no matter how excellent their line of attack, it would only prove successful if the commands ensuing from those that could see the whole picture were then put into action by those who could not – by the soldiers in the thick of battle itself. Even today, when soldiers have no idea how the overall battle is going they must trust their commanders' decisions in preference to their own inclinations.

God can see the whole picture in a way we shall never comprehend, but do we trust Him? When Christ asks us to do something, when He prevents us from having something, when He sends us somewhere we'd rather not go – do we trust the wisdom, knowledge and purpose of His decision? Do we trust that He loves and cares for us? Do we trust that as He can see the whole picture of the battle we're in, He must know the most effective course of action? Do we really trust God to provide for our immediate or long-term future? 'Never will I leave you; never will I forsake you' (Heb. 13:5).

But trust is only one element of obedience to God; for the submission of our steps to the Holy Spirit will ultimately depend on whom we really love.

'Love' provokes all manner of thoughts, dreams, memories and emotions: candlelit dinners, moonlit walks, hours on the telephone, unexpected gifts, a dozen red roses, sparkling champagne, a bunch of wild flowers, a picnic in the rain; tending a fevered brow, washing dirty laundry, digging up the brambles, putting out the bins, feeding through the night time, kissing away the tears, taking time to listen, talking through the fears; touching the untouchables, giving to the poor, visiting the prisoner, sharing when we've more, offering a listening ear, a shoulder to cry on – with no condemnation, love shares the pain.

But loving God is all of this and more; it swells within when we discover an intimate, spiritual connection, it flows from the heart through melodic, adoring songs of praise, it finds expression through the unconditional care of and concern for family, friends and society, but its sincerity is proved through our obedience to His commands.

Obedience. It's that word again, still carrying the austere image of reluctant resignation to authority. Certainly, if we considered submitting to a tetchy drill instructor, a strict teacher, an abusive husband, an overbearing father or a tyrannical leader, obedience might stem from intimidation, grudging obligation or outright fear. Jesus, however, links obedience with love. Not God's love for us, which is unchanging, but that which attests to the authenticity of our love for God.

Jesus' monumental victory over Satan was secured through obedience, the hallmark of His life despite its agonising climax – pure and perfect submission to His Father's will. Even though Jesus lived in enemy territory, Satan had no hold on Him because He loved His Father and always did exactly what He was asked (John 14:31).

Jesus taught that obedience demonstrates love, and the word He used was *agape* (John 14:15–15:17); one which implies we choose to love regardless of how we feel. In other words, Jesus didn't expect us to wait for feelings of love; rather, that we would esteem the One who loved us so much He was willing to save us through His own excruciating death. 'Greater love has no-one than this, that he lay down his life for his friends' (John 15:13). If we truly appreciate the Lord's great act of love our natural response will be to love Him – to obey His commands – in return. 'We obey God, not out of duty or fear or compulsion, but because we *love* him and trust that he knows what is best for us' (Rick Warren).[2]

Satan hates our loyalty to God. He'll do anything to tempt us away from obedience to God's Word and the Spirit's guidance. He'll use any device he can to deceive us into thinking that our way is better, easier or more profitable than God's. Of course we'll slip up from time to time but we are saved by grace, not by being perfect. So, rather than being immersed in the discouragement of blowing it again, let's focus on why we're going to keep trying to walk in step with the Spirit; not to earn God's favour, nor to earn salvation, but to please the One we love, who loves us unconditionally for eternity. After all, 'No-one serving as a soldier gets involved in civilian affairs – [they want] to please [their] commanding officer' (2 Tim. 2:4).

Training to work as a team

'Make every effort to keep the unity of the Spirit through the bond of peace' (Eph. 4:3).

It's important that we take our personal training seriously, but God still needs an army of soldiers working together to deal a major blow to enemy forces. With this in mind, I was interested to read that within the first week of British Army training, cadets are paired off in a 'buddy' system, reiterating this need to work together.[3] Even physical training develops this vital quality. Assault courses are recognised tests of strength but even the fittest soldier, attempting to navigate the 800m of muddy obstacles, stands no chance of success without learning to work as part of a team.

Teamwork is essential as it pulls together skills and trades to fight the same cause. The infantry can't say to logistics, 'I don't need you' – how else will they get supplies or transport? Officers can't say to communications, 'I don't need you' – how else will they deliver commands? One soldier can't say to another 'I don't need you' – how else will they achieve victory against the enemy line, how else might they get cover as they run, how else will they get help if they fall?

'... God has combined the members of the body ... that there should be no division ... but that its parts should have equal concern for each other' (1 Cor. 12:24–25). As an army we shall be successful in battle only as we work together. It's impossible to conquer a stronghold while we're firing in all directions and it's easier for Satan's snipers to take a shot at a lone straggler than a wounded soldier encircled with support from his or her comrades.

Are we isolating ourselves from Christian company? Are we pushing ahead with our own agenda without dovetailing into the whole? God is calling us back into His powerful, protective fold because the strength of His army will only be as strong as our heartfelt unity.

Dissension in the ranks can be expected from time to time. But when such disagreements result in festering pain and whispering cliques of opinion, the resultant disunity has the potential to weaken a unit's strength, create ineffective battle strategies and may even dissolve a whole army – may even split a church. It's happened many times in the history of world armies, and it can still happen in God's. Until we forgive others for any pain they've caused we create a mini battlefield within the larger one – a battle not with Satan but between ourselves. And so he sits back and scoffs at us while we do his job for him, cutting each other down with hurtful remarks or critical gossip, forgetting that 'Every kingdom divided against itself will be ruined, and every city or household divided against itself will not stand' (Matt. 12:25).

We may disagree with someone on a particular point but we can still live in harmony as we grow in humility, gentleness and patience, bearing with one another in love as we uphold the bond of peace that unites us in Christ (Eph. 4:2–3). And so let's consecrate our hearts and minds to hear and obey our Commander's instructions, regardless of each other's imperfections, for 'Without harmony in the State, no military expedition can be undertaken; without harmony in the army, no battle array can be formed' (Sun Tzŭ).[4]

Training ... for life

'So do not throw away your confidence; it will be richly rewarded. You need to persevere so that when you have done the will of God, you will receive what he has promised' (Heb. 10:35–36).

The energy and motivation to pray, the ease of wearing God's armour, the confidence to take our stand against Satan, the effectiveness of using our sword and the ability to discern Satan's strategies, all develop as we take our training seriously and for the long-term. If our nations' troops require such fastidious basic instruction and ongoing specialised training, how much more should we diligently pursue godliness, obedience and unity? And there's no better place to start than at home.

My immediate family probably see me at my worst; the tired irritability, the disgruntled sulks, the impatient snappy remarks and critical spirit. Acquaintances, however, generally see a much sweeter side of this imperfect woman. We may find it easier to be loving, patient and kind towards folk whom we relate to and get on with but I wonder if we don't also tend to let down our guard with those to whom we feel close. Family and friends provide an important training ground to develop God's holy ways, as much as our encounters with other imperfect people who've the knack of raising our hackles every time we meet!

Not one of us is perfectly disciplined to walk in obedience with the step of the Holy Spirit; perfectly trained in the ways of godliness, perfectly obedient to Christ, perfectly united in all our relationships. But we're all in the enemy's warpath – right now – regardless of how prepared we feel. He's got us in his viewfinder. He's got his spies analysing our weak spots and making the most of every opportunity to bombard them; to kick us when we're down; to whisper lies into our ear; to tempt and then to accuse; to pour on deceit and condemnation, if we'd but let him. So let's not lapse in the training that strengthens, equips, prepares, teaches and builds us up in our most holy faith to take our stand against the foe; a lifetime of training to be a soldier in God's army.

For reflection

• Has God been disciplining an area of your life recently? How well are you responding?

• Are you merely reading God's Word, or acting upon its instruction and doing what it says?

• If God's command to your heart clearly disagrees with the requests of others, or even your own ambitions, who would you actually obey; who do you love more?

• Do you feel too vulnerable or proud to draw alongside fellow soldiers within the safety of God's sovereign command? If so, ask God to help give you the courage and humility you need; after all, your fellow soldiers need you.

• Are you fighting a private battle with someone – whether they realise it or not? If so, take the time to name the person in prayer, to acknowledge that you need to forgive them, and to ask the Holy Spirit to help you through that process.

- In the film, *The Last Samurai*, Captain Algren was taken prisoner by Japanese Samurai. During his captivity he observed their daily habits, especially those of their swordsmen warriors, remarking that he had never before seen such dedication and discipline to perfecting one's skills.[5]

  - If someone were to spend a few weeks observing your life, would they remark that they had never before seen such dedication and discipline?

Let's pray …

Lord, I admit there are times I'm more interested in the healing and fulfilment of my inner being than I am in the disciplines of being transformed into Your holy likeness. What do You need to hone in my life, Lord? 'Search me, O God, and know my heart; test me and know my anxious thoughts. See if there is any offensive way in me, and lead me in the way everlasting' (Psa. 139:23–24).

Chapter 4

The armour of God

'Finally, be strong in the Lord and in his mighty power.
Put on the full armour of God so that you can take
your stand against the devil's schemes.'
Ephesians 6:10–11

Paul was under house arrest – chained to a Roman soldier. Not being one to give in to self-pity, however, or let adversity distract him from fulfilling God's purpose, Paul set about writing a letter to the young Church in Ephesus. He wrote about faith, salvation, spiritual blessings, purpose, power, tasks, relationships and the Church. Furthermore, he encouraged the Ephesians to be filled with God's Spirit and to live a life of love; a life befitting God's holiness, worthy of God's call, united with other believers and fulfilling God's work. Why else but '... for the praise of his glory' (Eph. 1:12).

But Paul knew from personal experience that if his readers acted upon his message they would invite ferocious attack – and that not merely from human beings but from invisible spiritual forces of evil. Turning to face his captor, what an enlightening image inspired his concluding encouragement: a Roman soldier prepared for battle, dressed in first-century armour (Eph. 6:10–17).

Armour isn't worn for fun, fashion or just when it takes our fancy; armour is worn as defensive covering, protecting the body from potentially harmful circumstances. Tortoise shells, thermal bodysuits, gas masks and metal-plated military tanks each serve as effective armour, defending against hungry dogs, sub-zero temperatures, mustard gas and bomb blasts. But just as chain mail won't protect against nuclear fallout and gas masks won't guard against bullets, so each soldier needs to wear appropriate armour according to the nature of their enemy. Facing a spiritual foe, therefore, we must wear spiritual protection.

Paul's letter taught about Christian life 'in Christ' (Eph. 1:3; 2:10,13; 4:32), concluding with the instruction to be strong 'in the Lord and in his mighty power' (6:10). It's a timely reminder that the training we considered in the last chapter isn't just a good idea, it's essential for effective warfare as our means to remain 'in the Lord'. Perhaps we imagine putting on armour like dressing in front of a mirror, but it's not that kind of activity. Rather, it's a continual abiding in Christ. It's only as we remain 'in' Christ that we can put on the armour of God; as we respond to the Spirit's training, as we seek to obey His commands and live in unity with other believers.

Jesus said, 'Remain in me, and I will remain in you … apart from me you can do nothing' (John 15:4–5). Apart from Christ, we cannot wear God's armour. Christ is our only means of defence and attack against the demonic realm. But as we remain in His mighty power, clothed in God's armour, we'll still be standing at the end of the battle – and not just standing passively enjoying its protection, but using it to oppose and resist the enemy, ultimately casting him out. 'The night is nearly over; the day is almost here. So let us put aside the deeds of darkness and put on the armour of light' (Rom. 13:12).

The belt of truth

'If we claim to have fellowship with him yet walk in the darkness, we lie and do not live by the truth' (1 John 1:6).

Paul described the elements of God's armour in the same order that Roman soldiers put theirs on, and must have noticed the pride soldiers took in their wide leather belts, studded with polished metallic mounts. In fact, they were regarded as a status symbol, invariably worn off duty to distinguish them from ordinary citizens while demonstrating, on duty, their readiness for battle.

The belt had a practical function too, as it protected the kidneys and was fundamental to wearing the rest of the armour; it tightened up the loose folds of the soldier's tunic enabling him freedom of movement, it fixed the breastplate in place and from it hung the scabbard in which the sword was sheathed.

Ephesians 6:14 translates from the Greek as 'Stand therefore having girded your loins with truth'. It sounds a bit old-fashioned, but 'girding' is used metaphorically with regard to being prepared, and from it we get our word 'girdle' describing anything that surrounds or encircles. So being prepared for spiritual battle requires that we live within (or encircled by) God's truth.

Just as Roman soldiers protected the cleansing function of their kidneys, we too must guard the ongoing cleansing of truth to our inner being. Reading God's Word and aligning our lifestyles to its decrees enables us to live within the power and protection of this belt – it teaches us how to remain 'in Christ'.

Are you wearing His belt with pride, living up to its values both in public and in private? And don't forget, we can't put on the rest of the armour without it!

The breastplate of righteousness

'Therefore, [sisters], we have an obligation …' (Rom. 8:12).

Although legionaries and higher-ranking officers may, at the time, have worn scale armour, Paul's Roman captor could well have been wearing a coat of chain mail; alternate rows of solid wire and riveted links, dropping just below the waist – an effective protection for the upper body and, more importantly, the heart. Although it was heavy (approximately 10kg) and susceptible to upward thrusts, it was comfortable as it followed the bodyline and enjoyed some weight transfer from the shoulders to the waist (via its attachment to the belt).

Paul recognised that to protect the Christian heart from Satan's evil schemes requires a covering of righteousness, one that is only found 'in Christ' but impregnable to every accusation Satan throws at us (past, present or future); for 'God made him who had no sin to be sin for us, so that in him we might become the righteousness of God' (2 Cor. 5:21). Nevertheless, the way we live our lives should prove Satan's accusations a lie (1 Pet. 2:12). Receiving the protection of Christ's righteousness implies we no longer live according to the sinful nature but seek to live according to the Holy Spirit – and that's how we effectively put on the breastplate.

To ignore the Spirit's conviction of inappropriate conduct is dangerous. Paul warned Timothy it could ultimately shipwreck faith (1 Tim. 1:18–19), and it would certainly leave a vulnerable spot in our spiritual protection. For Satan will try to condemn us, but provided we sincerely confess the things we do wrong, and seek to walk in heartfelt repentance, we'll find confidence to stand and defeat his every attack. And so we wear Christ's righteousness fixed to the belt of truth, held in place as we live as children of light; our lives consisting of good, right and truthful behaviour (Eph. 5:9).

Feet fitted with the gospel

'... established and firm, not moved from the hope held out in the gospel ...' (Col. 1:23).

Just before Christmas 2005, I enjoyed my first attempts at ice-skating beneath a star-filled sky at London's Somerset House. Wobbling towards the ice rink on a metal blade felt precarious to say the least, but I soon realised they were far better suited for standing on ice than my dainty evening shoes! And so, as I put my trust in those unfamiliar boots, my nerves settled and I grew in confidence, letting go of the barrier to join the flow of festive fun.

Marching and fighting on rough, muddy or rain-washed terrain, Roman soldiers relied on their boots to keep them standing upright while carrying heavy equipment or wielding a sword. These standard military issue *caligae* comprised three layers of tanned hide, laced upper straps and hob-nailed outer soles, providing the enduring support, flexible movement and rigid grip required.

Just as bladed boots prepared me to stand on ice and *caligae* prepared soldiers to stand on slippery ground, so the shoes of God's armour prepare us to stand in the spiritual realm of battle. When we trust in the awesome news that we've been saved from sin and death and reconciled to God through the blood of Jesus Christ, Lord and King over all creation, we have an unshakeable platform on which to stand. It's tempting to reach out for other props – good works, Bible knowledge, parrot-fashion prayers and so on – but fitting our feet with that gospel truth is our only means to stay upright and secure.

Satan knows the strength of this defence so he'll try to intimidate, confuse, mock or condemn our beliefs, but we can stand firm against him if we're prepared by the gospel truth. And that then prompts us to take up our shield of faith.

The shield of faith
'who through faith are shielded by God's power ...' (1 Pet. 1:5).

Facing his enemy, the Roman soldier crouched behind a large rectangular or oblong shield. Made from two pieces of wood fixed together with bull's hide glue, the shield (approximately 0.7m wide x 1.3m high) was bound in leather and edged with metal. The topside curvature enabled him to glance at the action while a metal boss covering the central hand grip deflected any barrage of spears or stones.

It was also common in that era of warfare to set alight pitch-dipped arrows before firing them from bows; a Roman soldier would have been out of his mind to face them without the defence of his shield, manufactured in such a way (and often dipped in water) to absorb the darts and extinguish the flames. And yet, I wonder what we do when the enemy attacks us with fiery darts of temptation, criticism, condemnation or injustice – darts that have power to penetrate our lives then wreak incalculable damage? It may not feel natural to hide ourselves behind something invisible but this is the nature of Christian life. 'We live by faith, not by sight' (2 Cor. 5:7). To take up our shield of faith is to put our complete trust in Christ and His deliverance from evil, no matter how forceful the attack may appear.

We can't stop Satan shooting arrows but we can take up our God-given defence. It protects us from the onslaught and, in so doing, extinguishes Satan's attempts to ignite fear, worry, greed, retaliation, unforgiveness, disunity, self-doubt and so on – a powerful weapon in disarming our foe.

And let's not forget how Roman soldiers stood side by side, with shields locked as an impenetrable wall, pushing against the frontline to take enemy ground. I trust this marvellous image might inspire us to live in unity in submission to High Command, that we too may use the united power of our shields to block Satan's works on a far larger scale.

The helmet of salvation

'O Sovereign LORD, my strong deliverer, who shields my head in the day of battle – ' (Psa. 140:7).

Roman soldiers were obliged to keep looking smart, so Paul may have seen his reflection in his captor's gleaming bronze helmet, designed to protect the whole of the vulnerable head. The headpiece attached to cheek and neck pieces and was tied under the chin by means of a leather thong. This passed through rings behind the ears which attached to a rivet on the underside of the neck guard making it virtually impossible to remove without the soldier's consent.

But by the time he was kitted out and holding his shield, he lacked enough hands to reach for his helmet. That's why Paul explains that to 'take up' the shield (from the Greek *analambano*), is the soldier's responsibility, but to 'take' (*dechomai*) the helmet (and the sword) implies receiving it from an armour bearer. We have a choice to take up the shield of faith but having done so, we simply have to receive our helmet of salvation. And as the tense in Ephesians 6:17 implies, we must continue receiving it until our hope is finally fulfilled and we're delivered from evil for ever (Phil. 2:12; 1 Thess. 5:8).

Head protection is vital. Satan assaults our thought-life in an attempt to discourage and deceive us into earning our salvation or making wrong choices – his choices. But Scripture provides some helpful advice: Firstly, that we fix our thoughts on Jesus and what He endured to save us from sin, so that we will not grow weary and lose heart (Heb. 3:1; 12:3); secondly, that we rely on God's Word and wisdom to direct our thoughts and decisions which help us stand in His victory (for example, Psa. 119:105).

The enemy will keep trying to penetrate our 'helmet' with lies, but remember he can't remove it. No one is immune from feeling discouraged, dejected and battle-weary but as we centre our thoughts on Christ and fill them with God's Word, He will guard our minds from doubt and lead us in His way of salvation. So, let's consciously decide that we won't consent to dwell on Satan's deceit and discouragement, but we will keep our thoughts 'in Christ'. Let's 'demolish arguments and every pretension that sets itself up against the knowledge of God, and [let's] take captive every thought to make it obedient to Christ' (2 Cor. 10:5).

The sword of the Spirit
'Jesus answered, "It is written ..."' (Matt. 4:4).

Dressed for battle, a soldier then needs the all-important weapons and Paul's gaze rested upon his captor's *gladius*; a double-edged stabbing sword wielded by the infantry, approximately 7cm wide and 50cm long. Its long tapering point proved particularly effective for stabbing – for fatal penetration – as opposed to the swing, strike and slash approach of longer, one-edged swords.

We too have a powerful weapon, 'the sword of the Spirit'. And as its name suggests, it must remain under the Spirit's operation if it's going to be effective in the spiritual realm. This sword of the Spirit is the *rhema* word of God (Eph. 6:17); the Holy Spirit-inspired word for each and every occasion.

When Jesus was led into the wilderness to face His enemy, He used the truth of God's Word to slay every temptation that Satan tried using as bait. Such was the power of defeat that the devil then left Him (Matt. 4:11); at least, for a little while! In defence against sin and in attack against Satan's kingdom, we've a mighty weapon to defeat his onslaught, time and time again.

But the power stems from the Spirit's control of the sword. We can't simply pick out scriptures of our own choosing for they have to be inspired for every battle we face. Our role is simply 'to stand', to wait and listen for the Spirit's guidance then to take – to receive – His word, and declare it with authority.

Please don't misunderstand me. Proclaiming truths from

God's Word should be a priority in our personal prayer-life as it builds us up in our faith (Jude 20), which in turn helps prepare us for battle. But quoting bits of the Bible won't in itself hurt Satan any more than shouting defiantly at him. It's the confident declaration of God's inspired truth that is potent with power to disarm and demolish the devil's devices with devastating success. And to do that, we must learn to listen, obey and use the strategy of divine High Command. That's why Paul encouraged the Ephesians to 'pray in the Spirit on all occasions' (Eph. 6:18). Prayer warfare does not consist of praying with our own mind or praying as we think we understand the situation but praying in the Spirit; praying as the Holy Spirit leads us, armed with the truth of God's inspired Word. (We shall take a further look at prayer in Chapter 6.)

'Therefore put on the full armour of God …' (Eph. 6:13)

In this ongoing battle with Satan's dominion we need every piece of God's armour; we need to be entirely clothed with Christ. It begins with the belt of truth and is completed as we sheathe our sword back into that truth, honed and at hand to wield at the Spirit's direction.

But I wonder how often we've fought the enemy without it, relying perhaps on our own sense of goodness, sincerity, ability or prescriptive ritual prayers. Human strategies have no power or protection in the spiritual realm but, while Satan's intellect is far greater than ours, he cannot and will never succeed in confrontation with Christ, who lives and works through submitted lives by the power of the Holy Spirit. Amen!

For reflection
• •

- In a world which compromises God's holy standards, in what ways do you find yourself in a battle to uphold His truth? If you're struggling, would it help to spend more time in God's Word to equip you with the knowledge of what truth really is?

- Do you ever give in to temptation knowing that you can confess and receive God's forgiveness later? Next time it happens, remember how it may leave you unprotected against enemy fire.

- Have you a tendency to lose confidence in the gospel message when faced with highbrow scientific argument or intellectual debate? If so, start reading and declaring aloud passages such as Ephesians 1:3–10, Philippians 2:5–11 and Colossians 1:15–23 on a daily basis. You may be surprised how much more confident you feel when next you face your opponents; not because you'll quote these texts in your arguments but simply because of the secure spiritual foundation built into your conscience on which you will stand.

- How do you normally respond to darts of temptation, criticism, condemnation or injustice fired at your life? Do you give in, retaliate or cower under guilt, worthlessness or insecurity? Next time those darts zip your way, guard your heart with your shield of faith, declaring the relevant truth from God's Word and responding in line with the fruit of the Holy Spirit (Gal. 5:22–23).

- In what ways does Satan battle for your mind? In what areas do you find your thought patterns distracted from God's will, at odds with God's Word or diluting the truth of God's love and salvation? Read and respond to Philippians 4:8 to build up your defences.

- In 2 Samuel 24:9 we read: 'Joab reported the number of the fighting men to the king: ... there were eight hundred thousand ... who could handle a sword ...' Could *your* sword skills be included in God's spiritual army?

- In Bernard Cornwell's historical novel *The Lords of the North*, hero Lord Uhtred reluctantly uses his battle skills to fight for King Alfred against the invading Danes. His armour was cumbersome but, as was customary in that era, he wore it in leisure-time as well as in battle, and as he grew accustomed to its weight it began to feel like a second skin.[1]

  - We too need to grow accustomed to wearing God's armour, whether we wake up to a diary filled with leisure, work or an outright battle. At what time each day could you spend a few minutes reflecting on the meaning of each piece of the armour, allowing the Holy Spirit to help you make necessary adjustments, in order to keep you 'in Christ'?

Let's pray ...

There is none like You, Lord. Holy Spirit, set my sights on the magnificence of Jesus in His armour of light that I might daily be inspired to remain in Him and enjoy His divine protection.

Chapter 5

Know your enemy

'How long will the enemy mock you, O God?
Will the foe revile your name for ever?'
Psalm 74:10

My heart aches when I hear news of military personnel caught up in air strikes, mortar attacks, 'friendly fire' incidents and the inevitable killings of armed combat; knowing full well that someone else's father, daughter, husband, sister, has worn their military uniform for the very last time.

It's one thing to write about spiritual battle from the tranquil solitude of my comfortable study, but I don't live with the constant worry of a loved one on the frontline. I can't even begin to imagine the emotional and physical hardships endured by these soldiers and I feel indebted to those who risk their lives for my peace, freedom and the welfare of the oppressed in this war-torn world.

There remains, however, an enemy whose universal warfare is common to us all and which carries eternal consequences. If I should underestimate him it could prove a deadly mistake. So let's take a tip from the experts who employ watchmen and reconnaissance personnel to assess their opponents: their size, location, strategy, skill and familiar battle terrain. Only then can they make ready their ranks with adequate men and equipment and, as we follow their example, we too can make ready and prepare ourselves for battle against our spiritual foe.

The prince of this world

'... the devil has been sinning from the beginning ...' (1 John 3:8).

I wonder if folklore has damaged our perception of Satan's power, with its image of a red-horned, long-tailed, cloven-footed being, holding a pronged fork in his wart-infested hand. As ugly as it is, it portrays him as a cartoon figure, seemingly irrelevant to 'the real world'; something or someone we can choose to believe in or dismiss. And perhaps that's exactly what he wants us to do! It wouldn't surprise me if outwardly he is in fact rather beautiful – Lucifer; the bright morning star – and perhaps that's why his rebellious ways can feel so tempting and attractive to our flesh-life. But no matter what he looks like, one thing is certain: inwardly he's not just ugly with evil, he's hideous and vile, an abomination of sin. And God's enemy – our enemy – should never be underestimated.

From Genesis to Revelation we see evidence of Satan's intellectual and supernatural powers and capabilities. He is the supreme power over the demonic realm and he controls the fallen world (1 John 5:19). In fact, he is 'the prince of this world' (John 12:31), 'The god of this age' (2 Cor. 4:4); 'the unseen power behind all unbelief and ungodliness'.[1]

Satan is the adversary (that's what his name means in Hebrew). He constantly challenges and opposes God. Since first he entertained dreams of grandeur and power, Satan grew to hate anything that reflected the Lord and set himself up as His rival. Neither has that hatred diminished, being further enraged and infuriated when Christ defeated his power over death through His victory on the cross. And so Satan still seeks to be god in our lives, scheming for our attention that we might choose his rebellious ways.

Satan is a deceiver (2 Cor. 2:11). He would rather we reject all things spiritual and unseen than put our trust in Christ for the salvation of our souls; he would prefer we remain indifferent towards him than worship God with sacrificial devoted hearts. And perhaps this touches on the very essence of his deception, for we don't have to be demonically possessed to be in his dominion and under his control. Satan works his evil guile through the unsaved sinful nature; he'll gain footholds and build strongholds, even in the lives of Christians if we let him (although I do not believe a Spirit-filled Christian can be totally possessed – that is, under the complete control and influence of the demonic realm).

Satan is a murderer and the 'father of lies' (John 8:44); that is his native language. As Christians, it's hard to understand why anyone would actually bow the knee and worship him, knowing that in doing so they also acknowledge the existence of God. But if one were deceived into thinking Satan might yet be capable of universal power and authority, that he could offer the carnal positions and possessions we crave, fulfil our sensual desires and promise to protect and provide for us, then it's not so hard to understand why Satanists exist; folk who've tragically fallen for his gargantuan lies to the utmost extreme. And it begs the question whether we've not fallen for some of his subtle lies ourselves; those which undermine the security of our salvation, the core of our self-worth, the perfect character of God or the nature of His unconditional love.

Satan is a tempter (Matt. 4:3). He deceives us into believing his lies then tempts us to respond in ways that rebel against God. We can't blame Satan for the things we do wrong, for we all choose how much we satisfy the cravings of our fallen nature. But we do need to stand up to him. He might be a bully but he can't overrule our choice to keep in step with the ways of the Holy Spirit.

Satan is the accuser (Rev. 12:10), and lives up to his name, 'devil', which means slanderer. He likes nothing better than to tempt us to sin through deceit and lies – then accuse us. Hurling exaggerated slander at us, he'll immerse us in condemnation; a state of overwhelming shame and guilt that feels impossible to escape.

Satan, indeed, is a master strategist, one who devises cunning schemes to try and bring us down (2 Cor. 2:11; Eph. 6:11). And let's not forget that he knows God's Word – possibly better than we do; he'll seek to distort its truth in order to promote his own version of reality in line with his evil schemes. He's both clever and relentless in his attack, but if we remain alert, there's no reason why he should catch us unawares.

The ruler of the kingdom of the air
'For our struggle is not against flesh and blood ...' (Eph. 6:12).

Although Satan's angelic body limits him to being in one place at a time, he is 'the ruler of the kingdom of the air' (Eph. 2:2); he governs a hierarchy of rulers, authorities, powers and spiritual forces of evil attempting to dominate the earth (Eph. 6:12).

I write about 'Satan' attacking us as it's a common turn of phrase, but to be absolutely correct, one should refer to the attack from Satan's dominion; the oppression of one or more of his spiritual forces of evil – fallen angels in league with the devil, whom we now call demons.

Demons effectively execute Satan's strategies. By tempting, tormenting, oppressing and even possessing individuals, they fulfil their master's bidding to exert control through humankind, to mar the image of God in His people and to lead them away from His truth. Where permitted, they have powers to control a person's mind and speech (Mark 1:23), to afflict sickness (Job 2:7) and crippling (Luke 13:10–11), to cause deafness, muteness (Mark 9:25), blindness (Matt. 12:22), seizures (Matt. 17:15,18) and to bring about acts of destruction (Job 1:12–19), to name but a few. Even the expressions of our sinful nature, if seen in their extreme, may occasionally be the manifestation of demonic oppression on someone's life (drunkenness, sexual perversion and licentiousness, for example, although we must never assume this without absolute confirmation from the Holy Spirit's discernment).

Nor is Satan's realm disorderly. Amongst the multitudes of demons, there appear to be principalities; those given higher rank and rule, some of whom may govern specific regions (Dan. 10:13). But whatever the exact nature of Satan's kingdom, all its participants have supernatural abilities in this spiritual war, seeking to use human life as instruments to fulfil their rebellious plans.

And so, demonic activity does not merely reside in eerie mysterious happenings. Much of our daily battle will be against the simple outworking of Satan's evil character in action against God's righteousness: hate opposing love; greed opposing self-control; despair opposing hope; resentment opposing forgiveness, and so on. So let's consider two key ways by which he exerts his influential control: first by gaining footholds, and then by building strongholds.

Footholds

"'In your anger do not sin": Do not let the sun go down while you are still angry, and do not give the devil a foothold' (Eph. 4:26–27).

A foothold is a secure position. It might be a ledge or hollow in which a climber can fix his foot; it could be an opportunity in the arena of work or art from which a budding talent may make further progress – and it's also the opening of sin in our lives that permits Satan a hold or influence and from which he might gain more control.

I mentioned above that we can't blame all of our sin on demonic temptation, for we were born with an inherent sinful nature (Psa. 51:5; Eph. 2:3); one which continues to harbour its own evil desires (James 1:14). But if we give in to sin – if we smoulder with anger, if we lack self-control, if we permit lust to ravage our sensual cravings, then it won't go unnoticed in the spiritual realm.

'... the devil prowls around like a roaring lion looking for someone to devour' (1 Pet. 5:8). As soon as we give him the slightest opportunity, he'll pounce – and make use of the chance to multiply the effects of the sin. If we persist in unrighteous anger, he'll encourage divisive argument and bitter estrangements; even to the point of dividing Christ's Church. If we persist in gluttony or drunkenness, he'll further the downward spiral of fleshly addiction, attacking the spiritual fruit of self-control and abusing the gift of our physical body; the temple of God's Spirit. If we seek increasing satisfaction of our sensual appetites, he'll provide the willing partner, appropriate porn or perverted ideas to poison Christ's beauty and purity within; breaking hearts, abusing trust and pouring on shame in the process.

Christ imparts His righteousness upon the believing soul, eradicating any claim Satan had on us. But there's a danger in unconfessed or persistent cycles of sin which permit the enemy an opportunity to exploit it, to inflict damage in our lives and, invariably, the lives of others. So let's develop the discipline of living in the opposite spirit: when tempted to deceive, let's choose to speak the truth; when tempted to criticise, let's choose to encourage; when tempted to be rude, let's choose to be kind; when tempted to hate, let's choose to show love; when tempted to resent, let's choose to forgive; when tempted to be greedy, let's choose moderation. 'Do not be overcome by evil, but overcome evil with good' (Rom. 12:21).

Temptation isn't wrong, but it's when we give in and indulge selfish cravings that we give the devil a foothold – his prime opportunity to use our sinful nature as a tool to permeate his ungodly ways, in and through our lives. But when we choose to put off that old self and live according to the opposite Spirit of God – in all goodness, righteousness and truth (Eph. 5:9) – our lives will be filled to ever-increasing measure with His holy characteristics.

Have you given the enemy a foothold in your life? Don't despair, for sincere confession will release his grip, repentance will oust him out, and walking in step with the Spirit will provide the guard on that 'gate' against potential further invasion. Seeking to live a godly life is more than a means to being *nice* Christians; it's strategic warfare in the battle for God's kingdom of righteousness against Satan's dominion of evil. After all, give Satan an inch, and he'll try to take much more; allow Satan a foothold and he'll start building a stronghold.

Strongholds

'For though we live in the world, we do not wage war as the world does. The weapons we fight with are not the weapons of the world. On the contrary, they have divine power to demolish strongholds. We demolish arguments and every pretension that sets itself up against the knowledge of God, and we take captive every thought to make it obedient to Christ' (2 Cor. 10:3–5).

A 'stronghold' is another word for a defended place, such as a castle with its solid stone walls, moat, drawbridge and ramparts from which to shoot arrows or pour boiling oil. Satan builds such strongholds. He defends people's minds from the invasion of God's truth using his spiritual influences of doubt, deceit, unbelief, idolatry, impurity; he imprisons cultural attitudes using power, greed, violence, immorality, materialism, and so on.

'The god of this age has blinded the minds of unbelievers, so that they cannot see the light of the gospel of the glory of

Christ, who is the image of God' (2 Cor. 4:4) – but he also builds strongholds in believers' lives where given permission to do so. Do you need to break out of a stronghold: fear, low self-esteem, unbelief, for example? See it for what it is – contradiction of God's truth, nothing more than that. Then face up to it with the sword of the Spirit which cuts through lies and compromise. Declare in faith your worth and identity in Christ in defence against oppressive condemnation, ask the Holy Spirit to strengthen your resolve to follow His ways and to grant you discernment of Satan's ongoing schemes.

I should perhaps mention that mental and emotional strongholds won't always tumble overnight, so be prepared to persevere with these strategic measures on a daily basis, always relying on the Holy Spirit's guidance for your specific situation. For as Jesus said, 'If you hold to my teaching, you are really my disciples. Then you will know the truth, and the truth will set you free' (John 8:31–32). So, trust in the Lord's promises, and watch that pretence of a prison wall start to crumble and fall.

This may prove more difficult when interceding in prayer on behalf of someone else and it's essential we never assume the nature of a stronghold without the Spirit's confirmation. Nevertheless, under divine direction, I believe we can rumble the foundations with prayer and declaration, although they will have to take that final step of faith to knock down the walls for themselves.

I'm aware that some readers might have known about these things for some time but still feel constricted by a lie, fear or addictive cycle. If that's you, then recognise the nature of the enemy behind the problem and take determined steps to activate truth into your being that in turn will set you free. After all, we've been given divine weapons to demolish these unstable fortifications built from delusions, lies and deceit, so let's 'Be self-controlled and alert. ... Resist him, standing firm in the faith ...' (1 Pet. 5:8–9). And if needs be, let's call on the help of discerning friends to care for and to pray for us, as we see this through.

Don't switch off the light yet!

'... in all these things we are more than conquerors through him who loved us' (Rom. 8:37).

Spending any time considering Satan's powers and the spiritual forces of evil is by no means my favourite occupation. In fact, where normally I work in silence, I've been playing praise music while writing this chapter; anything to lift my spirit above the ugliness of focusing on his character and the tangible sense of distracting oppression from the spiritual realm. So if you're reading this book in bed, please don't switch off the light just yet as I don't want to leave you dreaming of only one side of the story!

Satan is powerful, but only so far as God permits (Job 1:12; 2:6). Moreover, there may be times when God will use him to further His own purposes (Judg. 9:23; 1 Sam. 16:14; 1 Kings 22:20–21), or even to refine our faith (2 Cor. 12:7–9). What we must focus on, as Christians, is the need to be sensitive to the Spirit's leading us into specific repentance concerning the sin which gave the enemy entrance in the first place.

In the context of battle, however, in the arena of spiritual warfare to which we have been called, remember – we are more than conquerors.

A healthy respect for Satan's powers should certainly deter us from dabbling in the occult or using our own techniques to try and take his ground. But rest assured that we have been equipped to battle in Christ's authority with armour and weapons empowered by His victory on the cross. And this we do as we stand against Satan's temptations to compromise the godly life of Christ, and as we're led into prayer warfare by our Sovereign Lord – He who identifies the specific warring forces against us then guides us in each unique method of attack.

Is Christ living in you by His Holy Spirit? Then be encouraged, for you have nothing to fear. Although our enemy is powerful, He who is in us is far, far greater than he who is in the world (1 John 4:4).

For reflection

- What perception have you harboured of Satan and the demonic realm? Has it swung to the extremes of over-confidence, fear or disinterest? If so, are you willing to ask the Holy Spirit to give you a more balanced perspective?

- In what ways have you encountered the character of the demonic realm expressed through lies, deceit, accusations, fear or ungodly schemes? How have you, or would you now, stand against them?

- He who exercises no forethought but makes light of his opponents is sure to be captured by them.
  Sun Tzŭ[2]

- If you've made light of the enemy's influential power over godlessness, you may find yourself in the grip of a foothold or imprisoned by a stronghold. Have no fear but have every determination to cast him aside and claim your freedom in Christ, in accordance with His Word and accompanied by heartfelt repentance.

Let's pray ...

Father, it is good to have been reminded of the nature of the enemy but I continue to praise You, all-powerful Sovereign Lord, for the enabling power of Your Holy Spirit to overcome the devil's schemes in the spiritual realm.

Chapter 6

Prepared for spiritual battle

"'Not by might nor by power, but by my Spirit."
*says the L*ORD *Almighty.'*
Zechariah 4:6

L acking confidence is a common problem and one that I'm not immune to. I was painfully shy from the earliest age right through to married life. Although using my gifts in obedience to God has often nudged me out of my comfort zone, there are times I still withdraw into myself as if locking an invisible, self-protective gate. Peering out from behind this defence, I can watch the activity around me without taking part.

And that's probably where the enemy prefers me to be. I've no doubt there have been times when he's homed in on my personal insecurity and I've failed to stand my ground – compromising the truth of my Christian faith, grieving the Spirit's holy standards, failing to witness to an unsaved soul, keeping my mouth shut when I needed to declare God's Word or express the Spirit's burden in prayer in the hearing of other people; in the hearing of evil spirits over whom I might otherwise take authority.

So whether our confidence is stolen through insecurity and shyness, or misplaced in good works, natural talent or Christian maturity, let's take a moment to consider the source of authentic confidence that equips us for spiritual battle.

Know your authority

'I have given you authority … to overcome all the power of the enemy; nothing will harm you' (Luke 10:19).

When I married, I put aside my maiden name and adopted my husband's name, Le Tissier. From that moment I was authorised to hold a passport, sign cheques and withdraw cash in his name – and I wasted no time in doing so! Similarly, when we're adopted into God's family, we're permitted to use the authority of Christ's name (Mark 16:17). But do we?

It's an awesome truth that Jesus, who has been given all authority in heaven and on earth, indwells us by the Holy Spirit, delegating His authority to heal the sick (Luke 10:9), cast out demons (Luke 10:17) and defeat Satan's schemes (Luke 10:19). But having authority doesn't refer to the power itself, it refers to the right to exercise that power; a right that we may confidently claim when we believe in and remain in Christ.

Acts 19:13–16 describes the horrific consequence of unbelievers trying to invoke His authority to drive out evil spirits; they were overpowered and given such a beating that they ran away naked and bleeding. But even as believers we oughtn't to take our privilege lightly, rather we're obliged to honour that authority with appropriate behaviour; a painful lesson that Joshua had to learn …

Israel had grown accustomed to victory – even winning battles where the odds were stacked against them. But it all went wrong at Ai where they suffered humiliating defeat at the hands of a weaker army, compelling their confused and anxious leader to cry out to God. God's stern reprimand is a caution to us all: '… I will not be with you [in battle] unless you destroy whatever among you is devoted to destruction. Go, consecrate the people …' (Josh. 7:12–13). Israel had disobeyed, keeping something for themselves which ought to have been given to God (6:18–19). Unless they realigned their lives to His ways, they would not succeed against their foe.

Such is the direct relationship between submitting ourselves to God's ways and overcoming the devil's attacks; between remaining in Christ and growing in confidence to claim the authority that is rightfully ours. Satan had no hold on Jesus. Christ suffered cruelly at the hands of men, but Satan had no power or influence to use against Him in spiritual battle. And neither can Satan overrule us as we keep realigning our lifestyles, attitudes and behaviour to that of Jesus; for Christ's righteousness will be our armour and Christ's authority will empower our mode of attack.

I'm sure we're all eager to minister in the same divine power that Jesus did, but are we as enthusiastic about consecrating our lives in order to do so? It's certainly a question that challenges me. But Jesus taught that loving obedience is the environment God seeks to further empower our lives (John 14:23; 15:4); imperfect lives that are nevertheless energised, guided and ultimately fulfilled through communing with our Father in submissive, selfless prayer.

Take your stand …

'Therefore put on the full armour of God, so that when the day of evil comes, you may be able to stand your ground, and after you have done everything, to stand. Stand firm then …' (Eph. 6:13–14)

From the little I've observed watching the occasional war film, battles appear to be a torrent of action: commanders rallying the ranks with tribal war cries, troops charging, clashing shields and slashing swords, soldiers fighting one-on-one, others running for cover, horses galloping through the frontline or rearing up on hind legs, unexpected ambush from the rear, shouting, screaming, trumpet calls and cries; gunfire and bomb blasts, tanks moving stealthily forward, fighter jets roaring overhead … So how do we play our part? Where's the action? What should we do?

Paul answers that question quite simply, 'Stand … And pray' (Eph. 6:14,18). Warfare in the spiritual realm isn't concerned with racing about, shouting or even cowering or running for cover – it's about standing confidently in the spiritual realm in the authority Christ has given us. He grants power to withstand Satan's onslaught, He provides the way to stand without giving up an iota of ground and He gives us His strength to keep on standing against our relentless foe.

Three times in just two sentences Paul reiterates the need to stand, but where are we in this fight of faith? Do we feel like Saul and the Israelites who, when faced with Goliath's heckling, were 'dismayed and terrified' (1 Sam. 17:11)? Are we cowering beneath the enemy onslaught, vulnerable without adequate protection; racing back and forth across the battleground trying to dodge arrows but lacking the right weapon to retaliate; running in the opposite direction offering our back as an easy target?

If so, then let's take a tip from David who put his confidence in God, declaring boldly to the Philistine, 'You come against me with sword and spear and javelin, but I come against you in the name of the LORD Almighty, the God of the armies of Israel, whom you have defied. … All those gathered here will know that it is not by sword or spear that the LORD saves; for the battle is the LORD's, and he will give all of you into our hands' (1 Sam. 17:45–47).

When we recognise the battle belongs to the Lord then all we need do is appropriate His victory. So let's 'Fight the good fight of the faith' (Tim. 6:12), revived by the Spirit, protected in God's armour, secure in Christ's victory, trained by His hand upon our sword.

… And pray

'And pray in the Spirit on all occasions with all kinds of prayers and requests. With this in mind, be alert and always keep on praying for all the saints' (Eph. 6:18).

Putting on the armour enables us to stand in the spiritual battle but prayer focuses our attention on that spiritual realm; it keeps us within earshot of our Commander-in-Chief, and sustains our dependency on His presence and power for success – something the disciples understood after failing to help a demon-possessed boy. Asking Jesus why on this occasion their previous success eluded them, He replied, 'This kind can come out only by prayer' (Mark 9:14–29). According to my Bible commentary 'The disciples had apparently taken for granted the power given to them or had come to believe it was inherent in them. Lack of prayer indicated they had forgotten that their power over the demonic spirits was from Jesus.'[1]

Prayer isn't just something we do; prayer is an expression of our dependence on God. It forms words on our lips and groans from our hearts, it provides discernment to our spirits and is further empowered through the obedience and discipline of our flesh-life. In fact, Scripture encourages us to never stop praying: 'pray continually' (1 Thess. 5:17), 'Devote yourselves to prayer' (Col. 4:2), 'Be ... faithful in prayer' (Rom. 12:12), teaching us that everything – every situation, activity and incident in life – should be dealt with in prayer, thereby maintaining our link with the unseen reality of life. But this kind of constant, active prayer necessitates practice to develop untiring 'prayer-muscles'. It takes commitment to stay alert (Eph. 6:18) and maintain a constant watch (Matt. 26:41); it demands perseverance when emotions are low, circumstances difficult, energy dipping or we simply lack motivation. And we don't do that by sheer slog and striving, but only as we 'pray in the Spirit'.

Francis Foulkes writes, 'The Spirit is the atmosphere of Christians' lives, and as they live *in the Spirit* grace will be given to watch and power to continue in prayer.'[2] So let's be encouraged to pray in harmony with the Spirit as we reject our own opinions and thoughts, for '... the Spirit helps us in our weakness. We do not know what we ought to pray for, but the Spirit himself intercedes for us with groans that words cannot express. And he who searches our hearts knows the mind of the Spirit, because the Spirit intercedes for the saints in accordance with God's will' (Rom. 8:26–27).

We're in a spiritual battle and therefore dependent on the Holy Spirit's power; it's only as we stop telling Jesus what we think He ought to do and start asking Him to show us what He wants to do that we can then pray with faith in His name.

Praying in the name of Jesus implies two things: 1) that the prayer is motivated for and by God's purpose and character, and 2) the prayer is prayed by a believer sincerely seeking to submit to His holy ways and will. To tag 'in Christ's name' at the end of a prayer is not some kind of magical talisman, guaranteeing the response we hope for, but if we learn to pray in the Spirit by following His lead and keeping our lives in step with His ways, then we shall pray prayers in Christ's name that are powerful and effective.

I'm sure we want to see souls saved from Satan's dominion of death and darkness but let's not simply rely on the charisma or words of a preacher, the outreach events of an evangelist, the work of our youth leaders or the friendships we build with our neighbours. All these may be necessary but it's our stand in prayer in the spiritual realm that releases the power for the preacher, the evangelist, the youth worker and friend to break through spiritual blindness and strongholds.

Prepared to suffer
'... If they persecuted me, they will persecute you also ...' (John 15:20).

An eerie darkness veiled the noonday sun, silhouetting His pain-contorted body heaving against the bloody wooden cross. Was it really just five days since He rode jubilantly into Jerusalem? The disciples were devastated; terrified at this sudden turn of events.

'It is finished,' Jesus cried with His final breath.

Unable to comprehend that Jesus was fulfilling God's purpose and defeating Satan in the spiritual realm, the disciples ran – they hid – they locked themselves away.

When physical circumstances belie unseen spiritual reality we may well respond in like manner, for the repercussions of Satan's final death throes continue to abound. As immorality and violence engrave their hallmark on society and Christian persecution rises with alarming rapidity all over the world, 'Consider him who endured such opposition from sinful men, so that you will not grow weary and lose heart' (Heb. 12:3). There's nothing easy or comfortable about living in a war zone but countless men have marched into battle feeling cold, wet, fearful, exhausted and hungry – and so might we as we depend on the Spirit for strength.

There are times when spiritual victory is manifested in the physical realm: a healing, an unbeliever coming to faith, a release from demonic possession. But it isn't automatically partnered in this way. Jesus told us to expect trouble (Matt. 24:9; John 16:33) and countless folk who've been saved will nevertheless suffer the direct attack of Satan or the indirect consequences of the fallen world; victimisation, painful or terminal illness, financial hardship, violence and so on. Satan seeks to use these means to distract or harass our warfare and our trusting obedience of God, but we can choose to seek God's perspective on our minefield of difficult circumstances; to find strength in Christ and rejoice in His Sovereign purpose as we appropriate His victory in prayer.

I don't pretend that's easy; in fact, it may feel impossible to perceive personal tragedy as '... light and momentary troubles ...' (2 Cor. 4:17). And that's not to mention what others endure through chronic poverty, the sex-slave trade, famine or conflict, for example. But we have to make a choice. Either we believe and take heart from Scripture and our '... eternal glory that far outweighs them all' (2 Cor. 4:17) or we don't. I won't pretend I've got it all sorted but the following verse inspires the attitude I'm aiming for, meanwhile seeking to help those in need with prayerful support in the spiritual realm and practical support in the physical realm, as far as I am able.

> 'And we know we are going to get what's coming to us – an unbelievable inheritance! We go through exactly what Christ goes through. If we go through the hard times with him, then we're certainly going to go through the good times with him! That's why I don't think there's any comparison between the present hard times and the coming good times.'
>
> Romans 8:17–18, *The Message*

Jesus never promised worldly peace, He promised peace that the world cannot give – inner, spiritual peace and wellbeing; reconciled to God for eternity (John 14:27). The peace we may find in the world is temporary and fickle, but Jesus' peace is available today and every day for eternity, as many women will testify.

When my father left the family home after thirty-five years of marriage, my mother suffered an agonising period of readjustment. She recalls quite clearly how she simply could not have coped without knowing Jesus. She says:

I coped because I believed in what I'd read in the Bible …
and I clung on to God's promises for provision, help and
comfort, if only by the ends of my fingertips! I also believed
that according to His Word, He had a plan for my life from
its beginning to its end (Jer. 29:11), so that meant He still had
a purpose for me during that awful time. I scribbled down
every verse He inspired to my heart and chose to believe them.

Mum then explained what helped her to believe in those
scriptural promises for herself, opening her Bible at Psalm 91:
'If you make the Most High your dwelling – even the LORD,
who is my refuge – then no harm will befall you, no disaster
will come near your tent' (vv. 9–10).

That's what I did. I chose to make the Most High my refuge.
It's one thing to know it in your head, but you have to
really believe it to make it a reality in your heart. I can still
remember those first few agonising days after he left; I used
to sit for hours, frozen by numbness as my world caved in.
But in reality, God was ministering to me. There was stillness
within – I knew God was with me. In simply being still
before Him, He gave me His promised peace.

I also talked with a friend, recently widowed through her
husband's cancer; tearful, grieving, yet radiating peace
from the inward assurance that God is with her. His Spirit is
strengthening her and providing both the inner rest she needs
through her grief and a sense of hope for the future. And so I
could continue with stories of women who've suffered unjust
suspension from work, who've agonised over children mixed up
in all kinds of trouble, who've lost their health and consequently
their ability to work or socialise, who've given their hearts to

Christ at the cost of losing family and home – all of whom witness to the truth that though we live in a fallen world, though we experience heartache, difficulty and persecution for our faith, there is peace to be had and strength to be given to appropriate the promise of Christ's victory through prayer.

Therefore, my friends, 'Do not be anxious about anything, but in everything, by prayer and petition, with thanksgiving, present your requests to God. And the peace of God, which transcends all understanding, will guard your hearts and your minds in Christ Jesus' (Phil. 4:6–7).

> 'Where, O death, is your victory? Where, O death, is your sting?' The sting of death is sin, and the power of sin is the law. But thanks be to God! He gives us the victory through our Lord Jesus Christ. Therefore, my dear [sisters], stand firm. Let nothing move you. Always give yourselves fully to the work of the Lord, because you know that your labour in the Lord is not in vain.
>
> 1 Corinthians 15:55–58

For reflection

• Do you lack motivation to consecrate your lifestyle, habits, attitudes and the way you fill your time? If so, take a few moments to reconsider the blessings of a life transformed by knowing and experiencing Christ's power and authority.

• Have you lost confidence in praying in the name of Jesus, perhaps because your prayers went seemingly unanswered? God always responds, even if it's 'no' or wait'. Is it possible the prayer spoken in His name did not actually match up with His will? If so, how might you now pray confidently about that situation again?

• Are you seeking but struggling to hear the Holy Spirit's guidance in prayer? Ask Him to reveal any sin that may yet be grieving Him, for as the psalmist said, 'If I had cherished sin in my heart, the Lord would not have listened' (Psa. 66:18). Let's not give room for wilful or hidden sins to quench the Spirit's fire (1 Thess. 5:19).

• Do you know God's inner peace in your physical suffering? If you already feel too broken to respond to what I've been writing, perhaps it might help to ask a friend to come and pray with you, like Jonathan, who helped David to find his strength in God at one of the bleakest points of his life (1 Sam. 23:16); someone who might encourage you and sit with you as you take time to be still in the refuge of God's all-embracing presence.

• Wrestling is one of the most fatiguing of all competitive sports. The pitting of skill and muscle against one's opponent in such sport is extremely demanding. This is the kind of battle we face with these invisible spiritual beings. The picture is one of close, demanding, fatiguing encounter … How tragic and heartbreaking it is to see believers reeling and staggering under Satan's assault with little hope of victory. The victory is already provided. It remains for us only to aggressively use it and not passively assume it. Mark I. Bubeck[3]

- Paul reminded his readers they were wrestling (translated 'struggle' in the NIV) against spiritual forces, not simply flesh and blood human beings (Eph. 6:12). Are you taking seriously the preparations for battle we've considered in this book? If so, you've possibly encountered disheartening opposition, but remember, it's only as we keep on training that our spiritual strength and stamina will increase.

Let's pray …

Lord, I cherish the moments of tangible spiritual intimacy in the solitude of Your presence and admit that these uplifting encounters are more attractive than wrestling in prayer. When my spirit is willing but my flesh feels weak, please bring to my mind Your perfect example in the Garden of Gethsemane, that I too may not give up but persevere in prayer.

Chapter 7

Learning from our ancestors

'Give us aid against the enemy, for the help of man is worthless.
With God we shall gain the victory,
and he will trample down our enemies.'
Psalm 60:11–12

During a recent Remembrance Day service, I was stunned to learn that in 3,400 years of global history there have only been 268 years of peace.[1] In fact, type 'war' into any internet search engine and you'll find plentiful historical statistics and ongoing estimates of military and civilian casualties; millions of untimely deaths in the twentieth century alone, with countless numbers of wounded and hoards of displaced refugees. It begs the question: haven't we learnt anything in 4,000 years to help eradicate warfare today?

The sad truth is that while the world remains in bondage to Satan, there will always be power struggles, disputes and internal conflicts. And that's not all, for our spiritual battle with unseen forces of evil will rage on until Jesus returns in His glory.

So we can't eradicate warfare. But, as officers study previous battles to help them win their wars, so we can learn from our own warrior ancestors. And to do that, we're going to look at six examples which relate to the previous chapters. I trust that our forebears' approach to battle might support what we've been learning and help us to put it into practice.

Chapter 1: To be or not to be … a soldier: Joshua 1:1–9

'… Now then, you and all these people, get ready to cross the Jordan River into the land I am about to give to them … I will give you every place where you set your foot, as I promised Moses' (vv.2–3).

The Israelites, long freed from Egyptian bondage, stood on the verge of a land God had already promised to them; a good and spacious land filled with fruitful vegetation – a land assuring abundant life. The promise was guaranteed but they still had to take possession of it. So, putting their trust in God, they obeyed His instructions and the tribe of nomadic shepherds learnt to fight and overpower the enemies in the land; to take hold of the life that was rightfully theirs as children of God.

Jesus makes a similar promise: 'The thief comes only to steal and kill and destroy; I have come that they may have life, and have it to the full' (John 10:10). Jesus freed us from bondage to Satan's captivity and promised us abundant life both now and in the future. But there are enemy spiritual forces at work that will try and prevent us taking hold of those promises and, like the Israelites, we must do something about it; we must fight for our rights in Christ.

As Christ's soldiers we'll need to take this warfare seriously if we want to experience the fruitful abundance of our divine inheritance: inner peace (John 14:27), security (Heb. 13:5–6), provision of what we need (Matt. 6:25–34), fulfilment (John 10:10), identity and worth (Acts 17:28), assurance (Jer. 31:3), rest (Matt. 11:28), acceptance (Luke 15:11–24), forgiveness (1 John 1:9), hope (Lam. 3:25) …

God is for you, the devil is against you; are you willing to take your stand in spiritual battle to claim that which you've been promised?

'Have I not commanded you? Be strong and courageous. Do not be terrified; do not be discouraged, for the LORD your God will be with you wherever you go' (Josh. 1:9).

Chapter 2: One world, two realms: 2 Kings 6:8–18

'"O LORD, open his eyes so that he may see." Then the LORD opened the servant's eyes, and he looked and saw the hills full of horses and chariots of fire all round Elisha' (v.17).

Israel cowered under threats of ambush from the king of Aram, but one night the enemy proximity felt too close for comfort. The city where Elisha and his servant were staying was surrounded by enemy soldiers. They were trapped – there was no escape – at least, that's the way it appeared while the servant focused on the physical realm.

Elisha, however, observed the physical realm from the perspective of the spiritual realm. He knew that the unseen reality of God's angelic warriors far outweighed the powers of mortal attack. And so he prayed that his servant would be able to see that reality for himself. Just imagine the servant's change in countenance when his eyes were opened to the fiery horses and chariots filling the surrounding hills!

Are you feeling anxious because of uncertain circumstances, an unfair situation at work, an oppressive number of problems and difficulties, a vindictive colleague or employer, for example? Ask God to help you discern if there is any spiritual force of evil behind these events, and to open the eyes of your heart to perceive your gargantuan protection and support in the spiritual realm.

If, however, you're already so embroiled in a gut-wrenching situation that you're finding it almost impossible to pray, let alone shift your focus to the unseen, then start by building up your faith and strengthening your soul with the promises in God's Word: "'Because [she] loves me," says the LORD, "I will rescue [her]; I will protect [her], for [she] acknowledges my name. [She] will call upon me, and I will answer [her]; I will be with [her] in trouble, I will deliver [her] and honour [her]'" (Psa. 91:11–15).

"'Don't be afraid,' the prophet answered. "Those who are with us are more than those who are with them'" (2 Kings 6:16).

Chapter 3: Army training:
Joshua 3:1–5; 5:1–6:25

'Joshua told the people, "Consecrate yourselves, for tomorrow the LORD will do amazing things among you." ... the LORD said to Joshua, "Make flint knives and circumcise the Israelites again"' (Josh. 3:5; 5:2).

On first hearing the Jericho story, I probably pictured the Israelites on the bank of the River Jordan, practising their battle skills for days on end – never quite feeling on a par with the trained strategists behind Jericho's walls; never quite believing their farming tools and ancient spears would match up to Jericho's swords. And perhaps they did, but that's not what clinched the victory.

God didn't say, 'Go for a ten-mile run, do a hundred sit-ups then hone your battle skills.' He said, 'Consecrate yourselves ... circumcise ...' The key to Israel's battle training lay in their willingness to obey God's holy commandments. That was the primary factor that enabled their limited skills and empowered their weaker army, for that was the means by which God would fight on their behalf.

Glimpses of God's eternal grace shine through many stories of the Old Testament but the Israelites remained subject to covenant Law, contrasting with the unmerited acceptance we enjoy through the fulfilment of God's grace in Jesus Christ. But that doesn't permit us to do our own thing. If you're new to the faith, you may feel inspired by the disciplines of godliness, obedience and teamwork. When we've followed the Lord for some time, however, there's potential for apathy, compromise and even self-righteousness to subtly sneak in. That's what happened to the Church in Ephesus to whom the Lord said, 'I know your deeds, your hard work and your perseverance. I know that you cannot tolerate wicked men ... You have persevered and have endured hardships for my name ... Yet I hold this against you: You have forsaken your first love' (Rev. 2:2–4).

Army training feels arduous unless we're motivated by love for Jesus. So if you're struggling to get inspired, perhaps it may help to diarise some quiet space and time out with God to reflect on His gift to you, His unconditional love, and to restore, refresh or reignite your relationship.

'The commander of the LORD's army replied, "Take off your sandals, for the place where you are standing is holy." And Joshua did so' (Josh. 5:15).

Chapter 4: The armour of God: 1 Samuel 17:20–50

'Then Saul dressed David in his own tunic. He put a coat of armour on him and a bronze helmet on his head. David fastened on his sword over the tunic and tried walking around, because he was not used to them. "I cannot go in these," he said to Saul, "because I am not used to them." So he took them off' (vv.38–39).

The Israelites were terrified of Goliath – a giant of a man with a sword and an ego to match. Not one of Saul's experienced soldiers was willing to take him on; only the shepherd boy, David.

Whether Saul offered David his armour out of kindness or in the hope of sharing the glory of victory, we cannot say for sure; but David refused it. With an oversized helmet slipping down his forehead and weighty body armour overhanging his young shoulders, it took all his strength just to stumble around the tent! As encouraging as it might have felt to face the enemy trying to emulate someone more experienced, and kitted out with their honourable attire, it would have been disastrous. Setting it to one side, David confidently faced his foe clothed with the impenetrable protection and equipping of God's power.

There was a time when I was impressed and influenced by folk who prayed against spiritual forces of evil in ways that appeared to be powerful but which, in reality, relied solely on expressions, opinions and methods that couldn't be backed up by a sound understanding of Scripture. Stumbling blindly, I took no ground in warfare while I tried to copy them. It was only when the Holy Spirit revealed the error to my heart that I shook off those things, and asked Him to empower me in His way.

There is no substitute for remaining in Christ. Have you unwittingly relied on anything but faith in and obedience to Christ's truth, righteousness, promises and Word to protect and equip you for battle? Then follow David's example and remove it from your thinking without further delay and go out, confident in the knowledge that Christ is your protection, and Christ's inspired Word is your sword.

'All those gathered here will know that it is not by sword or spear that the LORD saves; for the battle is the LORD's, and he will give all of you into our hands' (1 Sam. 17:47).

Chapter 5: Know your enemy: Joshua 2:1–24
'Then Joshua son of Nun secretly sent two spies from Shittim. "Go, look over the land," he said, "especially Jericho."' (v.1).

I make no apology for returning to Joshua; after all, he was quite possibly the greatest military strategist in ancient history. Here we're reminded that before he faced the enemy, he sent out spies to assess their equipment, numbers, courage and poise. Hiding in the house of Rahab the prostitute, whose spiritual insight was far more acute than that of her seemingly worthier neighbours, they gained the inside knowledge they required.

From time to time I invite the Holy Spirit to spy out the land of my life. I ask Him to show me what enemy forces may be oppressing me, whether I'm offering them easy footholds, and what, if anything, is keeping me bound from walking in the powerful and abundant life in Christ. And His response is always helpful, enabling me to face the onslaught with divinely-inspired strategies and the weapon of God's Word. We can also ask the Holy Spirit to give insight concerning Satan's schemes in, for example, the country where we live, providing discernment to empower our prayers against that which remains unseen.

The enemy isn't afraid of you but he is petrified of the power of Christ in you. Do you know the nature of the enemy forces currently bombarding your life? Do not be afraid to ask the Lord to show you, for then you'll be better equipped to stand against them and to live in the inheritance that is rightfully yours in Christ.

'They said to Joshua, "The LORD has surely given the whole land into our hands; all the people are melting in fear because of us"' (Josh. 2:24).

Chapter 6: Prepared for spiritual battle: Judges 20:18–48

'Then the Israelites, all the people, went up to Bethel, and there they sat weeping before the LORD. They fasted that day until evening and presented burnt offerings and fellowship offerings to the LORD' (v.26).

Of all the tragic stories in the Bible, this surely rates as one of the saddest. Not only was Israel at war, but at war with one of its very own tribes – the Benjamites – who'd failed to purge their ungodly wickedness that led to the horrific death of a Levite's concubine (see Judg. 19:1–20:16).

The tribes united to tackle the problem – 400,000 Israelite fighting men against 26,700 skilled Benjamites – and, on enquiring of the Lord who should first go up and fight, the tribe of Judah was selected. But despite their significantly smaller army, the Benjamites cut down 22,000 Israelites on the very first day. With much weeping the Israelites enquired of the Lord, and again were instructed to fight – this time losing a further 18,000 men (by now the Benjamites had defeated more swordsmen than they had themselves).

Once again, the Israelites wept before the Lord, but something was changing in their hearts; this time their tears were accompanied with fasting and sacrificial offerings. They'd known it was right to purge wickedness from their midst but perhaps they'd relied on their greater numbers rather than on the Lord; perhaps they'd prepared themselves for battle with mere physical training and a show of humility, rather than heartfelt, humble dependence on God?

Either way, the story highlights two important principles when entering battle. Firstly, the Lord's command to fight on behalf of righteousness, where wickedness would otherwise fester unchallenged, may yet have tragic consequences in this life. Present-day martyrs provide ongoing testimony of folk who stand up for their faith in oppressive regimes while losing their homes, families and, so often, their lives for doing so. We know they've won the eternal victory but the often painful process of death and the torment and grief suffered by their families should be enough to motivate our prayers and practical support.

Secondly, just knowing that something is right and feeling capable of doing it is inadequate preparation for battle. The power to overcome requires heartfelt repentance, humble dependence upon God's empowering and a sincere expression of our passion for His name. God may be nudging us to fast or make further sacrifices to equip us for battle, but are we willing to respond?

Fasting should never be considered a formula for guaranteed success, but there is much evidence in Scripture of the spiritual dependence and power with which it equips those who submit to its temporary physical discomfort. Ezra proclaimed a fast before the people journeyed through bandit-infested territory (Ezra 8:21–23); King Jehoshaphat did likewise when attacked by a superior army (2 Chron. 20:2–3); and our supreme warrior, Jesus, had been fasting in the wilderness before His famous encounter with Satan (Luke 4:1–13).

We might fast for other reasons aside of protection and power in warfare, and for different lengths of time, but if nothing else let's remain open and obedient to the Holy Spirit's prompting to do so (for there will be no use in fasting as a mere religious observance, Luke 18:10–14). There's nothing like a whetstone to sharpen the edge of a blunted blade; there's nothing like fasting to prepare ourselves for spiritual battle.

'And the Israelites enquired of the LORD. ..."Shall we go up again to battle with Benjamin our brother, or not?" The LORD responded, "Go, for tomorrow I will give them into your hands"' (Judg. 20:27–28).

Our valiant war cry

'With your help I can advance against a troop; with my God I can scale a wall. As for God, his way is perfect; the word of the LORD is flawless. He is a shield for all who take refuge in him. For who is God besides the LORD? And who is the Rock except our God? It is God who arms me with strength and makes my way perfect' (Psa. 18:29–32).

I referred above to King Jehoshaphat's battle with a vast army, a story which relates how Jehoshaphat appointed men to head up his ranks, singing praise to the Lord. And it was as they began to sing and praise that God set ambushes against their enemies who were subsequently defeated (2 Chron. 20:21–22).

What an awesome picture that paints! But let's not take it out of context with the whole story, for it was only after the people humbly sought the Lord that He confirmed His strategy for victory, which inspired the people to praise (v.17).

Praise, while being a natural response to promised success, is essential in battle in order to keep the eyes of our heart focused on Jesus rather than the enemy. Praise in itself is not a weapon of warfare but, when used appropriately, it fuels our faith – somewhat like a traditional war cry.

And so, as we draw our study to a close, envisage with me a historic battle scene just minutes away from onslaught. The commander-in-chief astride a magnificent stallion parades in front of his army, rallying his troops with cries of vengeance, victory and promise of rewards. In response, a soldier beats his shield with his sword, the rhythm swiftly spreading through the ranks. Charging into battle, their war cry strengthens fearful hearts, enthusing daunted morale … This is the place of praise; this is the time to take up a war cry – declaring our victory in Christ, building up our faith against the enemy's lies and boosting our morale to face any and every situation.

Our own High Commander surveys the world in the glory of His majestic splendour. His clothing is as white as snow, the hair on his head is white like wool, His eyes are like blazing fire, His feet like burnished bronze, His voice like the sound of rushing waters, His face like the sun shining in all its brilliance. Dressed in a full-length robe with a golden sash around His chest, out of His mouth comes a sharp double-edged sword (Dan. 7:9; Rev. 1:13–16). And He says, 'Do not be afraid. I am the First and the Last. I am the Living One; I was dead, and behold I am alive for ever and ever! And I hold the keys of death and Hades' (Rev. 1:17–18).

Have you bowed the knee in allegiance to God's army? Then arise with me, and declare in faith

> The LORD is my light and my salvation –
>> whom shall I fear?
> The LORD is the stronghold of my life –
>> of whom shall I be afraid?
> When evil men advance against me
>> to devour my flesh,
> when my enemies and my foes attack me,
>> they will stumble and fall.
> Though an army besiege me,
>> my heart will not fear;
> though war break out against me,
>> even then will I be confident.

Psalm 27:1–3

And so, my friends, let's venture into spiritual battle undaunted.

For reflection
• •

Each study in this chapter, relating to chapters 1 to 6, includes points to consider and respond to. Read them again if you've not had time to reflect upon their implication in your own life.

> ... the skilful fighter puts himself into a position which makes defeat impossible, and does not miss the moment for defeating the enemy.
>
> Thus it is that in war the victorious strategist only seeks battle after the victory has been won, whereas he who is destined to defeat first fights and afterward looks for victory.
>
> Sun Tzŭ[2]

I trust that from reading this book you feel more prepared and willing to take your stand against Satan's spiritual forces of evil, for as you remain in Christ, you secure your impregnable defence, and as you learn to live and pray in step with the Holy Spirit, you'll be making the most of every opportunity to take enemy ground. The victory has been won; now place yourself in position to take hold of it.

Let's pray ...
Lord, I hear Your war cry and I am not afraid, for this is Your battle. Help me each day to abide increasingly in You, and take my rightful stand against evil.

Notes

Introduction
1. *The Matrix*, Village Roadshow Films (BVI) Limited, 1999.

Chapter 1
1. Composed and written by Sir Andrew Lloyd Webber and Tim Rice, 1970.
2. Richard O'Connor, *To Be a Soldier* (Shrewsbury: Airlife Publishing Ltd., 1996), p.1.
3. Ibid., p.5.

Chapter 2
1. Having described the flood damage, I ought to mention that when we eventually made it up to the cottage, we were amazed and relieved to find that despite both our neighbours being flooded downstairs, we'd been remarkably (miraculously?) protected. We didn't suffer anything like our neighbours and were deeply grateful that at that particular time and for His own particular reasons, God chose to shield us from anything more than an inch of water in the lean-to at the back. Another day, another time, perhaps our experience will be different, for we are no less likely to suffer the problems of this fallen world than anyone else; but God is still worthy of praise.
2. Sun Tzŭ, *The Art of War* (London: Hodder & Stoughton, First Edition 1981, Revised Edition 2005), p.16.

Chapter 3

1. Richard O'Connor, *To Be a Soldier* (Shrewsbury: Airlife Publishing Ltd., 1996), p.19.
2. Rick Warren, *The Purpose Driven Life* (Grand Rapids, Michigan, USA: Zondervan Publishing House, 2002), p.95.
3. Richard O'Connor, *To Be a Soldier* op. cit., p.25.
4. Sun Tzŭ, *The Art of War* (London: Hodder & Stoughton, First Edition 1981, Revised Edition 2005), p.39.
5. *The Last Samurai*, Warner Bros. Entertainment Inc., 2003

Chapter 4

1. Bernard Cornwell, *The Lords of the North* (London: HarperCollins, 2006), p.81.

Chapter 5

1. Commentary in *The Compact NIV Study Bible* (London: Hodder & Stoughton, 1987), p.1733.
2. Sun Tzŭ, *The Art of War* (London: Hodder & Stoughton, First Edition 1981, Revised Edition 2005), p.61.

Chapter 6

1. Commentary in *The Compact NIV Study Bible* (London: Hodder & Stoughton, 1987), p.1481.
2. Francis Foulkes, *Tyndale New Testament Commentaries, Ephesians* (Leicester: IVP, First Edition 1963, Second Edition 1989), p.185.
3. Mark I. Bubeck, *The Adversary* (Chicago: The Moody Bible Institute, 1975), pp.71 and 77.

Chapter 7

1. Charles Burke (1975) quoted by Karl Ernst Nipkow, *God, Human Nature and Education for Peace: New Approaches to Moral and Religious Maturity* (Aldershot: Ashgate Publishing Ltd., 2003), p.129.
2. Sun Tzŭ, *The Art of War* (London: Hodder & Stoughton, First Edition 1981, Revised Edition 2005), p.25.

National Distributors

UK: (and countries not listed below)
CWR, Waverley Abbey House, Waverley Lane, Farnham, Surrey GU9 8EP.
Tel: (01252) 784700 Outside UK (44) 1252 784700

AUSTRALIA: CMC Australasia, PO Box 519, Belmont, Victoria 3216.
Tel: (03) 5241 3288 Fax: (03) 5241 3290

CANADA: David C Cook Distribution Canada, PO Box 98, 55 Woodslee Avenue, Paris, Ontario N3L 3E5.
Tel: 1800 263 2664

GHANA: Challenge Enterprises of Ghana, PO Box 5723, Accra.
Tel: (021) 222437/223249 Fax: (021) 226227

HONG KONG: Cross Communications Ltd, 1/F, 562A Nathan Road, Kowloon.
Tel: 2780 1188 Fax: 2770 6229

INDIA: Crystal Communications, 10-3-18/4/1, East Marredpalli, Secunderabad - 500026, Andhra Pradesh.
Tel/Fax: (040) 27737145

KENYA: Keswick Books and Gifts Ltd, PO Box 10242, Nairobi.
Tel: (02) 331692/226047 Fax: (02) 728557

MALAYSIA: Salvation Book Centre (M) Sdn Bhd, 23 Jalan SS 2/64, 47300 Petaling Jaya, Selangor.
Tel: (03) 78766411/78766797 Fax: (03) 78757066/78756360

NEW ZEALAND: CMC Australasia, PO Box 303298, North Harbour, Auckland 0751.
Tel: 0800 449 408 Fax: 0800 449 049

NIGERIA: FBFM, Helen Baugh House, 96 St Finbarr's College Road, Akoka, Lagos.
Tel: (01) 7747429/4700218/825775/827264

PHILIPPINES: OMF Literature Inc, 776 Boni Avenue, Mandaluyong City.
Tel: (02) 531 2183 Fax: (02) 531 1960

SINGAPORE: Alby Commercial Enterprises Pte Ltd, 95 Kallang Avenue #04-00, AIS Industrial Building, 339420.
Tel: (65) 629 27238 Fax: (65) 629 27235

SOUTH AFRICA: Struik Christian Books, 80 MacKenzie Street, PO Box 1144, Cape Town 8000.
Tel: (021) 462 4360 Fax: (021) 461 3612

SRI LANKA: Christombu Publications (Pvt) Ltd, Bartleet House, 65 Braybrooke Place, Colombo 2.
Tel: (9411) 2421073/2447665

TANZANIA: CLC Christian Book Centre, PO Box 1384, Mkwepu Street, Dar es Salaam.
Tel/Fax: (022) 2119439

USA: David C Cook Distribution Canada, PO Box 98, 55 Woodslee Avenue, Paris, Ontario N3L 3E5, Canada.
Tel: 1800 263 2664

ZIMBABWE: Word of Life Books (Pvt) Ltd, Christian Media Centre, 8 Aberdeen Road, Avondale, PO Box A480 Avondale, Harare. Tel: (04) 333355 or 091301188

For email addresses, visit the CWR website: www.cwr.org.uk

CWR is a Registered Charity – Number 294387

CWR is a Limited Company registered in England – Registration Number 1990308

Day and Residential Courses
Counselling Training
Leadership Development
Biblical Study Courses
Regional Seminars
Ministry to Women
Daily Devotionals
Books and Videos
Conference Centre

Trusted all Over the World

CWR HAS GAINED A WORLDWIDE
reputation as a centre of excellence for
Bible-based training and resources. From
our headquarters at Waverley Abbey
House, Farnham, England, we have been
serving God's people for over 40 years
with a vision to help apply God's Word
to everyday life and relationships. The
daily devotional *Every Day with Jesus* is
read by nearly a million readers an issue
in more than 150 countries, and our
unique courses in biblical studies and
pastoral care are respected all over the
world. Waverley Abbey House provides a
conference centre in a tranquil setting.

For free brochures on our seminars and
courses, conference facilities, or a catalogue
of CWR resources, please contact us at the
following address:
**CWR, Waverley Abbey House, Waverley
Lane, Farnham, Surrey GU9 8EP, UK**

**Telephone: +44 (0)1252 784700
Email: mail@cwr.org.uk
Website: www.cwr.org.uk**

Applying God's Word
to everyday life and relationships

Inspiring Women: True Confidence

Wendy Bray

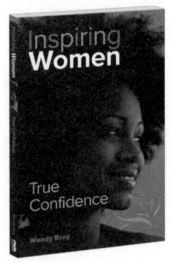

Find true confidence in your relationship with the Father, the Son and the Holy Spirit with these insights of biblical wisdom.

112-page paperback
ISBN: 978-1-85345-470-7

Available June 2008

Other Inspiring Women Books:
Finding Freedom – The Joy of Surrender

Helena Wilkinson

Discover the deepest joy and freedom possible – through the grace of deep surrender – and gain a closer walk with God.

112-page paperback
ISBN: 978-1-85345-451-6

Created as a Woman

Beverley Shepherd

Takes a fresh look at what it means to be a woman and to have the Lord's unconditional and unchangeable love, through biblical insights, personal testimonies and the author's own life experiences.

112-page paperback
ISBN: 978-1-85345-450-9

Price: £6.99 each

Prices correct at time of printing

Inspiring Women Every Day

Various authors

Daily Bible notes written by women, for women, to inspire and encourage all ages:

- Increase your faith and ignite your passion for Jesus
- Find practical support to face life's challenges
- Be enlightened by insights into God's Word.

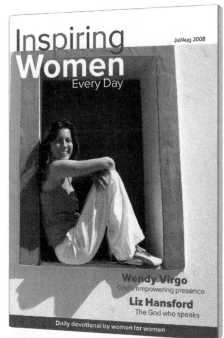

120 x 170mm, 64-page, bimonthly booklets
ISSN: 1478-050 X

Priced individually at £2.25 each

Only **£12.50** for a UK annual subscription (six issues)

How to be a Secure Woman

Jeannette Barwick and Catherine Butcher

Who loves me? Who needs me? What's the point of my life?

This eight-session study uses contemporary stories to enable you to:

- Discover where you seek security – and why you haven't found it
- Know with certainty that you are highly valued
- Gain the lasting security found only in a relationship with God.

Ideal for individual or group use.

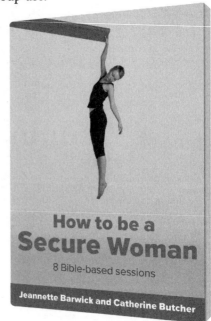

A6, 96-page booklet
ISBN: 978-1-85345-307-6
Just £5.99